"*The Plot Thickens* is a highly useful book that is written in an accessible style and filled with valuable examples."
—*The Writer*

"A crisply written, nicely detailed examination of the art of storytelling. Beginning writers will find plenty of practical tips and useful advice in its pages."
—*Booklist*

"Lukeman's personable writing style elevates *The Plot Thickens* from a text on writing to a written version of the mentor you always wished you could have."
—*The Midwest Book Review*

"Fantastic . . . gives you lots of insight on how to write a great story. We couldn't put it down. It was better than reading a great novel."
—Hollywoodlitsales.com

"My favorite kind of how-to-write book . . . never high-handed or stuffy, the book is easy to read but thought-provoking at the same time. . . . Lukeman's comments were very informative and insightful and could be used by all of us when it comes time to edit our novels."
—FictionFactor.com

"A book that deserves a prominent place on any writer's bookshelf."
—FictionAddiction.Net

"Lukeman uses his experiences as an agent to create a book that will benefit all types of writers. Film and novel critics will find Lukeman's book to be an outstanding guide when analyzing story plot."
—AbsoluteWrite.com

"So well written—so tight and polished—that it provides a perfect example of its own principles. . . . It would be a rare writer who didn't find his or her manuscript improving through application of Lukeman's extensive questions."
—TheCompulsiveReader.com (and NetAuthor.Org)

"One of the best how-to guides on the subject. I took notes; it's that good. He knows suspense and knows how to create and sustain it. . . . Read this book cover to cover, then put it in the resource section of your personal library. When tempted to lift actors from central casting, or to retread a tired old tale, reach for *The Plot Thickens* instead and build something good from the ground up."
—QuantumMuse.com

"Anyone who loves to write character-driven plots will love this book! . . . An easy to read book that can be read from start to finish, or which can be delved into whenever you're blocked for an idea on where your plot should go next, *The Plot Thickens* is a guide that will complement any writer's reference shelf."
—Womenonwriting.com

THE
PLOT THICKENS

ALSO BY NOAH LUKEMAN

The First Five Pages

THE
PLOT THICKENS

8 Ways to Bring Fiction to Life

Noah Lukeman

 St. Martin's Griffin   New York

www.stmartins.com

Design by Philip Mazzone

Library of Congress Cataloging-in-Publication Data

Lukeman, Noah.
    The plot thickens : 8 ways to bring fiction to life / Noah Lukeman.
       p. cm.
    ISBN 0-312-28467-5 (hc)
    ISBN 0-312-30928-7 (pbk)
       1. Fiction—Technique. 2. Plots (Drama, novel, etc.). I. Title.

  PN3378 .L85 2002
  808.3—dc21

                                                    2001058564

10   9   8   7

At the risk of repeating myself, I dedicate this, my second book, to my mother. I never planned to write another book on writing, and set down some thoughts on plot for her sake alone. Her encouragement brought forth a chapter, and before I knew it, it was too late to turn back.

Contents

Acknowledgments

Alicia Brooks brought life to this book. While I debated whether to write it, her genuine enthusiasm for the proposal left me no choice—an enthusiasm that hasn't waned since. I am lucky to have her as an editor.

I am equally indebted to George Witte for championing the proposal and providing in-house support. At St. Martin's Press, I'd like to thank my copyeditors, Sara and Bob Schwager; my jacket artist, Phil Pascuzzo; my production editor, Kevin Sweeney; my publicist, and Associate Director of Domestic Rights Lisa Herman for their excellent work.

As always, my family has been there for me, and I am deeply grateful for their support.

I thank Daniel Myerson for his historical consultation; Stella Wilkins and the Abner Stein agency for their steadfast support; Joel Gotler for his psychic abilities; and Michael Ovitz for giving me the autonomy to agent and write at the same time.

Introduction

People are always asking me if the university stifles writers. I reply that it hasn't stifled enough of them. There's many a best-seller that could have been prevented by a good writing teacher.

— FLANNERY O'CONNOR

The word "plot" can cause a great deal of trepidation in writers. This is chiefly because plot has become synonymous with having a "great idea," and the pressure to come up with such an idea can be stultifying. The very thought can breed a feeling of futility, since great ideas come and go with the whims of inspiration.

It is the purpose of this book to show that plot is not just about having a single great idea; on the contrary, a good plot is an amalgamation of many ideas or elements of writing, including characterization, journey, suspense, conflict, and context. An idea is paramount, but without these supporting elements, an idea by itself is just that—an idea, an abstraction, not a 120- or 300-page living being replete with shades, color, and texture. Most stories do not come in one flash—on the contrary, the best stories are organic to their characters, to their layers of suspense and conflict.

Contrary to what many popular books would like you to believe, there is no formula to assure a great or "classic" plot. There are no steps, paths, no things you must do, and no things you cannot do. This is not a book of rules and mandates. I would be wary of any such book. On the contrary, this book grapples, philosophically and practically, with age-old principles of story. If you glance at the table of contents you will not find catchy, gimmicky topics; on the contrary, it deliberately covers familiar ground—characterization, suspense, conflict. These principles have sustained works for thousands of years and can be found at the core of all great writing. This book differs in that it attempts to cover new ground *within* these topics, to offer examples you will not have seen, and to offer exercises you will not have previously considered.

Another purpose of this book is to inspire you with new ideas, whether you are revising your work or embarking on a new project. That is why this book applies equally to the beginning and advanced writer: It is no easier for the advanced writer to come up with ideas. And because it covers such broad principles, this book can apply equally to the novelist, screenwriter, playwright, nonfiction writer, and even poet. After all, the nonfiction writer should be concerned with suspense, as the screenwriter should be concerned with context, as the poet should be concerned with conflict.

Two caveats:

As I give examples, you'll find abundant references to films—more so than books. I do this because my chief concern is illustrating (sometimes abstract) points, and by referencing films there is a greater chance that more readers will recognize the reference. I also reference films because film is a medium that has devoted itself to plot, and I would be remiss to ignore them; I also want to show writers they can learn from everything, from *Moby Dick* to *M*A*S*H*.

Caveat Two: Chapters One and Two are the exceptions in this book. Chapters One and Two are essentially fleshed-out questionnaires, designed to help the writer explore character. As such, they are comprised of roughly 90 percent questions and 10 percent discussion.

This is not a safe book. It is impossible for you to read it and not walk away armed with a host of new ideas. It will push you to your limits, as it forces you to explore every last aspect of your work. As a Literary Agent, I have been pushed to mine, as I have had to read over fifty thousand manuscripts in the last five years alone. Now I will teach back what you taught me. Now I will return the favor.

Chapter One

Characterization: The Outer Life

Begin with an individual and you find that you have created a type; begin with a type and you find that you have created—nothing.

—F. SCOTT FITZGERALD

You may have been in a situation—perhaps in a government office—where you've been asked for your mother's social security number, your father's place of birth, and realized, in a horrific flash, that you don't really know the people you think you know best in the world.

How much more so is this true of the people you attempt to create out of sheer imagination, often on a whim, people whose very existence can be the result of a mere circumstance or plot twist. You have no opportunity to spend time with them as living, breathing people, to eat lunch, get drunk, play sports with them, watch them at work. You can only add imagination to imagination, picture how they might act in imagined circumstances and settings. In real life, though, when we anticipate, we are often wrong. Ultimately human beings are impossible to predict, and there are factors we just cannot anticipate.

To even begin to accurately bring a character to life on the page you must do your homework, quiz yourself fastidiously about every last detail of your character's inner and outer life. The seemingly insurmountable task of capturing a person on the page will become possible—even easy—once the details are laid out before you. Once you really know your character, your knowledge will flow unmistakably through the text; like an undercurrent, it will authenticate every word, gesture, and action. Without this knowledge, you are lost. As a writer, you have no visuals or audio to assist you. Only words on paper. Or, as Toni Morrison says, "only the 26 letters of the alphabet."

As character is the basis for all further talk of journey, conflict, suspense—and is the cornerstone of plot—we begin this book with the construction of character, which I cover in three chapters. This chapter, the first, is designed to quiz you on your knowledge of your character's surface (or outer) life. It will prompt you to consider facets you may not have previously considered. Write down your discoveries as you go.

I use "he" predominantly and "she" in instances where the facet is particular to a woman. Keep in mind, though, that all facets should be considered for both sexes; as I mentioned in the disclaimer, the use of "he" is solely a grammatical convenience.

Appearance

The biggest mistake writers make is feeling compelled to set down their character's physical appearance immediately, usually at the expense of the narrative. You can get to know someone without knowing what he looks like—by phone, by mail, on-line, through a confessional. Looks fade and even change, and people are not the sum of their physical parts.

It *is* important for you to know—for yourself—every aspect of your character's appearance, just not crucial to divulge it all to the reader, and certainly not right away (unless the story demands it). Ideally, you will leak a description, at opportune times (preferably earlier), in unique ways, and in palatable doses. Imagine the following four scenarios in helping you accurately portray your character:

Police Sketch

A murderer is on the loose. He has been terrorizing the city for months, but there is no living witness to offer a description. He strikes again, and this time you are there, get a good look at him before he flees. The city looks to you for an answer. Across from you sits a professional police artist. Behind you hover ten detectives, waiting. What does this man look like?

Appearance I

Face: What is his facial structure? Does he have elongated cheekbones? Wide, sturdy jaws? Broad forehead? A jutting chin, or no chin at all—or perhaps he's overweight and has three chins? Does he have wide, thick, brutal lips—or small, thin lips, pinched tightly together? A huge nose? A small one? Broad or narrow? Short or long? Are his eyes large or small? Close together or far apart? What color are they? Is he cross-eyed? A glass eye? Does one eye wander? What about his eyebrows? His eyelashes? Does he have any facial hair? A moustache? Beard? Goatee? Long sideburns? Is he tan or pale? What is his race? Does he have any deformities—any scars, moles, burns, injuries? Overall, would you consider this person good-looking?

Hair: Does he have any? What color? Is it long, short, curly, straight, wavy? Thinning, balding? Dyed? Healthy or unkempt? Tied back in a ponytail, hanging over his eyes, braided in dreadlocks?

Body: How tall is he? How much does he weigh? Is he fat? Skinny? Muscular? Are some body parts in better shape than others—does he have muscular arms but a big belly? Broad shoulders but skinny legs?

Age: How old is he? Is it easy or hard to tell? What physical signs of age are there? Wrinkles, crow's-feet, jowls, spots? Does he look prematurely old at twenty? Or like a teenager at forty-two?

If you had to say he looked like one person, who would it be?

Let's say the murderer is a woman. Some other questions might arise: Does she have large or small breasts? Her waist?

Hips? Legs? How does she keep her nails—bitten to the bone, perfectly manicured, painted black, fake extensions? Does she have long eyelashes, does she use mascara? Makeup? Does she wear too much? Not enough? Is she naturally beautiful?

If you had to say she looked like one person, who would it be?

Now, leaving the police room, apply these rigorous questions to the character(s) in your work. What details might you add that you may not have thought of previously?

If you were to ask your character his analysis of himself, would there be any discrepancy? Denial? Does he think he's handsome even though objectively he's not? Or, does he think he's ugly although he's good-looking? Does he consider himself young although he's obviously well aged? Does he think he's short although he's over six feet? Does she think she's heavy even though there's not an ounce of fat on her? What do any of these discrepancies say about the character? Do they point to any greater issue?

A Crowded Room

You've set up a friend on a blind date. You described what his date looks like, but he's now standing in the bar where they are supposed to meet, and there are over two hundred people and potentially many girls who fit her description. He calls you from a pay phone and needs to know more. He's already been there for twenty minutes and fears if he doesn't find her soon, they'll miss each other. What else can you tell him?

Appearance II

Clothes: What does she normally wear? Designer clothes? Work clothes? Casual? Salvation Army? Are her clothes generally revealing? Does she wear miniskirts and low-cut blouses? Or does she tend to cover every inch, wearing skirts down to her ankles and modest, oversize sweaters? Does she wear large straw hats, tie her hair back with bandannas? Accoutrements? Handbags, jewelry, watches? A ring on every finger? A large, golden cross about her neck? Large hoop earrings? A nose ring? A tattoo on her shoulder? Is she more likely to wear Rolex and Guccis, or sandals and a five-dollar watch off the street? Does she dress more expensively than she can afford, or does she dress down despite her wealth? What colors does she tend to wear? All black? Neon pink? Does she have a good sense of fashion? Are her clothes in line with the latest trend, or ten years out of style?

Grooming: Is she tailored, impeccably dressed, or an unkempt, unbathed slob? Does she shower twice a day, or once a week? Does she smell? Does she wear too much perfume?

Body language: Does she stand stiffly, or is she always slumped over? Does she walk in a feminine manner, swaying her hips as she goes, or does she walk like a man, as if looking for a fight?

Voice: Some people can be picked out of a room by voice alone. Does she have a forceful, booming voice? Can her conversations be heard across the room? Or does she talk in a whisper, hardly audible, so you always have to ask her to repeat herself? Is her voice high or low? Nasal and whiny, or clear? Is it the perfectly neutral, businesslike voice of a telemarketing professional, or is it the husky, suggestive voice of a prostitute? Does she talk with great speed, in a manic rush? Or does she beat around the bush, talking so slowly that you watch the clock as you wait for her to finish? Does she stutter? Have an accent? A lisp?

Now, leaving the bar, apply these rigorous questions to the character(s) in your work. What details might you add that you may not have thought of previously?

If you were to ask your character her analysis of herself, would there be any discrepancy? Does she consider herself in line with fashion while wearing outdated clothes? Does she think her voice is sexy though it is loud and piercing? Does she think her jewlery not fancy enough while wearing a gigantic diamond ring? What do these discrepancies say about the character? Do they point to any greater issue?

The Doctor

You are one of the top doctors in the country, and your specialty is diagnosing hard-to-name illnesses. You have just been referred your toughest case yet. He has been to ten doctors in as many months, and no one can find what's wrong with him. He sits across from you now on his first visit, ready for you to inquire into his medical history.

Medical Background

How is his general constitution? Can he not get sick in the middle of a jungle, or does he get sick within one hundred feet of someone's germs? Has he ever been seriously sick? With what? How many times? Was it hereditary? If not, how did he contract it (in a foreign country, sleeping with someone)? Was he ever hospitalized? What was that like? How much of an impact have his illnesses had on his life? How much do they have right now?

Does he have a chronic illness or condition? Is he on any medication? Asthma inhaler, blood pressure regulators, antidepressants? How often must he take it, and how does it affect his life? (For a diabetic, his illness—his constant monitoring of food, blood sugar, and injections of insulin—will be a major part of his life.) Are there side effects? Interactions? How must he compensate (not drink, not smoke, adopt a special diet)?

Has he ever been injured? How? (A sports injury, a fight, a car accident?) Broken bones? Plastic surgery? Bad back, tendinitis, arthritis? Does he have any disabilities? Is he blind, deaf, lame, mute, mentally challenged? Is he insane? Schizophrenic?

Now apply these questions to the character(s) in your work. What details might you incorporate that you may not have thought of previously?

If you were to ask your character his analysis of himself, would there by a discrepancy? Does he consider himself sick although he is perfectly healthy? Is he a hypochondriac?

The Psychologist

You are a psychologist, specializing in inter-family dynamics. You've just been referred a new patient and need to know everything about his family before you can begin.

Family Background

Was he raised by both parents? If not, why? Were they divorced? Was one deceased? How old was he when either of these things happened? If he wasn't raised by both parents, was he raised by his mother or his father? Or did he alternate between them? How much time did he spend with each? Did he live in different homes? Did they live close by? Or, was he raised by another relative (grandparent, uncle)? Was he raised by a homosexual couple (two fathers, two mothers)? Was he adopted? If his parents divorced, did either remarry? Does he have a stepparent?

What did his parents do for a living? How did that affect his upbringing? Are his parents still alive? How old are they? Is he close to them? How often do they talk? How much of an influence have they had on his life?

Does he have grandparents? Did they live close by? Did they have a big influence on his life? Are they still alive?

How many siblings does he have, if any? Being an only child could be a crucial aspect of a character's makeup, as could his having six siblings. Brothers or sisters? Has having five brothers made him more masculine? Has having five sisters made him more feminine? Is he the oldest, youngest, or middle child? How does this affect him? Has being the oldest made him more protective, paternal? Has being the youngest made him pampered, spoiled? How old are the siblings? Is he close to them? In competition with them? How often does he see them? Do they live close by? How big a role do they play in his life?

Is he married? At what age? For how long? How did they meet? Did they come together despite the odds? Is he happy? Is she? Are they equal as a couple, or are there discrepancies between them (in age, wealth, status, education, religion)? Are they able to overcome these discrepancies, or are they driving them apart? Do they fight? How often? What are their common interests (if any)? Where do they dissent? Do they treat the kids differently? Do they work together? Do they play a pivotal part in each other's lives? Or do they live in separate homes? Do they have a prenuptial agreement? Is either having an affair? With whom? For how long? Does the other know?

Does his wife have a large family? How do they get along? How big a part do they play in his life? Are his siblings married? How does he get along with his brother's wife? His sister's husband? How has marriage changed family dynamics? Do his siblings have children? How does he get along with their kids? Is he a good uncle? Are they all close?

Now apply these questions to the character(s) in your work. What details might you incorporate that you may not have thought of previously?

The Adoption Agency

Children

Imagine you work for an adoption agency, and a woman has just come through the door who wants to adopt an infant. You need to find out everything you possibly can about her current children (if any), fertility, and motives for adopting. What sort of questions might you ask?

If childless, does she plan on having children? Is she unable to get pregnant? Has she spent years visiting fertility clinics, to no avail? Is she on birth control? Did she have a permanent operation? Does she regret that? Does she worry about her biological clock?

If she has children, how many does she have? How many would she like? Or are these more than she wanted to begin with? Did she get pregnant by the first boy she slept with? Were her pregnancies rough? Her deliveries? Did she have any abortions? Lose any babies? Are they all hers by birth, or are some adopted, or some from another marriage? Does she resent them for it?

How old are her children? What are their names? Were they named after any relatives? How close is she to them? Do they cause her grief? Or do they bring her honor? Is she in competition with them? Are they attending the same colleges she did? How much of herself does she see in them? Does she consider herself a good parent? Do the kids? How does she treat her kids? Is she abusive? Has she ever hit them? Or is she abused by them? Do they listen to her? Does she listen to them? Does she live vicariously through them? What sacrifices has she made for them? Does she have grandchildren? Is she active in their lives?

Now apply these questions to the character(s) in your work. What details might you incorporate that you may not have thought of previously?

If you were to ask your character to analyze herself, would there be a discrepancy? Does she consider herself good to the kids while she hits them?

The Employer

Imagine you run a company and are responsible for hiring new employees. A critical position has just been vacated, and a candidate sits before you. The future of your company might lie in his skills and abilities. He is a complete stranger. What might you ask him?

Education

Consider not only the basics—whether he completed elementary school, high school, college, or graduate school—but also *when* he finished these programs (a Ph.D. at twenty-four is as telling as a B.A. at forty-eight). How is his grammar, diction, spelling, vocabulary? Is he smart despite having never been to school? Is he naive despite his Yale degree? How hard did he have to struggle to get his education? Did his parents pay for it, or did he work himself through college? How much does it mean to him? Does he act or feel superior as a result? Inferior?

Any special training? Does he have a commercial driving license? Training as an electrician, as a plumber? Does he take continuing adult education? Is he constantly seeking to educate himself? Does he study new languages or vocabulary words on his own? Is he a big reader? Is he the self-taught type, or does he need the structure of a program? Does he love to learn, or is all education a struggle?

Employment

What sort of job does he have right now? A white-collar job (executive, lawyer, doctor, banker), a middle-end job (bureaucrat, salesman, manager), a blue-collar job (mechanic), or a minimum-wage job (delivering pizza)? How long has he had this job? Someone remaining in the same job for forty years is as telling as someone switching jobs once a month. Is this job congruous with his background, his level of education, his training? Is he delivering pizzas with a Ph.D.? Is he running a major company with a high school diploma?

How hard (and how long) did he have to work to get to where he is now? Did he get help from parents, friends? Does he work for his parents? Is he in his parents' line of work at all? Is he in direct competition with his parents? Who are his competitors? Who are his clients?

How is he viewed within his company? Is he a slacker? Does he come in late, leave early, and take long lunches and vacations? Is he motivated, organized? Does he have a direct boss? How do they get along? Does he have people below him? How does he treat them? Is he honest in all his business dealings?

Does his job consume his life? Is it part-time, full-time? Is he a workaholic? Does he work three jobs? Is his role in business his main identity in life? Or is he unemployed? Between jobs? How many jobs has he had? Has he never been able to hold a job? Why not? Problem with authority? Police record? Or is he so rich he doesn't have to work?

Is she stuck at home raising kids when she wants to be out working? Does she experience sexual harassment at the office? Has she ever? Is she working in what is traditionally a man's field (i.e. policewoman, firewoman, stockbroker)? Is she treated with less respect because she's a woman? Is he working in what is traditionally a woman's field (i.e. hairdresser, schoolteacher)? Is he scoffed at because of it?

If he is not in a permanent or ideal job right now, what job does he aspire to?

If you were to ask your character to analyze himself, would there by a discrepancy? Does he consider himself a hard worker although he works four hours a day? Does he consider himself well thought of within his company while the people around him can't stand him?

Police Record

If you were to hire someone, you would probably run a background check, which would include a basic check of his criminal history. Has he ever been arrested? If so, how many times? How frequently? When was the last arrest? Was he convicted? Did he serve time? Where? For how long? Who bailed him out? For how much? Were his crimes violent (armed robbery, assault, rape, murder)? Or nonviolent (embezzling money, computer hacking, burglary, auto theft)? Why did he turn to crime? Was it a onetime thing? A mistake? An act of desperation? Or did he enjoy it? Is he a career criminal? Has he ever been in a car accident? Was anyone hurt? Does he have many tickets, moving violations? (There is a big difference between the man who has a blemish on his record for shoplifting as a teenager and the man who has a blemish for assaulting his ex-girlfriend.)

Now apply these questions to the character(s) in your work. What details might you incorporate that you may not have thought of previously?

The Banker

Your job is to approve mortgages. Your bank has been burned many times before, at the cost of hundreds of thousands of dollars, and you have been given the mandate to be extra cautious in approving someone new. An applicant sits before you. What might you like to know?

Economics

What's his credit report like? Spotless? Awful? Has he ever declared bankruptcy? Defaulted on a loan? Do creditors call his house night and day? Does he default on other things in life, too? Is he spending his life paying off debt? What percentage of his monthly bills does it comprise?

How much does he make? Is there any potential for growth? How much does he have in the bank? How much in investments, in collateral? How much in debt? Is he rich, poor, or somewhere in the middle? If rich, how long has he been wealthy? Did he earn it the hard way, or receive an inheritance? If poor, has he always been poor? Is there any hope of his being rich? If once rich, how did he lose his money? Is he a gambler (the stock market, horses, casinos)? Can he not stop himself from buying goods (fancy cars, electronics, clothes)? Does he have a credit card problem? Is he steeped in college loans? Supporting someone else? Living off someone else? Did he steal the money? How important is money to him? Does he live in perpetual anxiety over it? Or does he hardly care at all?

Was he raised rich? What was the neighborhood like? Destitute (ghetto), working class (mining town or fishing town), middle class (suburbia), upper middle class, or upper class (Beverly Hills)? How did his class affect his identity? Does he hate rich people? Despise poor people? What are his deep feelings about money and the people who have it?

Possessions

Make a list of the major things he owns. Any valuables? Jewelry? Artwork? Coins? Stamps? Rare books? Any collections? Expensive furniture? Electronics? Music? Musical instruments? China? Silverware? Plants? Is it a long or short list? What comprises the greatest percentage of it? What does that say about him?

How long has he had all of his stuff? Has he owned it all his life? Was it passed down from generations? Or did he just buy it all last week? Did he steal his things? Is he renting or leasing them? How much value does he put on his possessions? Does he take good care of his things, or does he treat them poorly, lose them? How big a role do they play in his life? Does he equate himself with what he owns? Or does he give everything away? (Also see Geography: Residence below.)

What about vehicles? Does he own a car, truck, motorcycle? Did he buy, rent, lease, or steal? How old is it? How long has he had it? How frequently does he get new vehicles? How does he treat them? Is he a good driver? Does he spend every weekend waxing his car? Or has he not washed it in ten years? How important is his vehicle in his life—does he equate it with who he is?

Now apply these questions to the character(s) in your work. What details might you incorporate that you may not have thought of previously?

If you were to ask your character to analyze himself, would there by a discrepancy? Does he insist money is unimportant to him while watching every cent? Does he consider himself having been raised humbly though he was brought up in Beverly Hills?

The Matchmaker

Imagine you work for the most elite matchmaking service in the country. Your clients are the wealthiest, most eligible bachelors in the world, and they, too busy to look for themselves, are completely trusting you to find them the match of their lives. What might you ask interviewees?

Romantic History

Has she ever been married? Engaged? If so, is she separated, divorced, a widow? At what ages did any of these happen? (Divorced at eighteen can be as telling as single at sixty.) How many serious relationships has she had? How many passing, casual relationships? How big of an impact have these partners had (or do they still have) on her life? Is she haunted by past boyfriends? Stalked by an ex-husband? Must she still see him once a week when he visits the kids? How frequently does she enter relationships? A new boyfriend once a month, or once every five years? Is she the one to initiate the breakup? How does she go about meeting men? Does she spend time in bars? Place ads in magazines? Does she enjoy life being single? Or is a relationship a necessary part of her life? What does she look for in a mate?

If you were to ask your character to analyze herself, would there by a discrepancy? Does she consider herself hardly ever in a relationship while having twenty boyfriends a year?

The Real Estate Agent

Imagine you are a successful real estate agent and a woman has come to you desperate for help in finding her the perfect place to live. She has no idea where she wants to move, and you know nothing about her. What might you ask?

Geography: Residence

Where does she live now? In a house, apartment, trailer, houseboat, tent? Does she own or rent? Or is she squatting, crashing at a friend's, or homeless? How long has she been there? (A person staying in one place for fifty years is as telling as her moving every week.) Is she a homemaker, and is every detail of her residence of the utmost importance? Or is she a slob, and is her residence in need of repair? Is her residence spartan or crammed with trinkets? Where did she live before? Is it a step up or a step down? Who does she live with, if anyone? A roommate, sibling, lover, parent, friend? Are there others in the building? On the block? Are they nuisances? Does she have rowdy neighbors? A Peeping Tom? Is she rowdy herself? Does she honor leases? Does she damage her abodes? What does she aspire to in a living situation?

You can tell much about a person by her home. Furniture, books, music, art—take a look around. What's there? You can tell a lot simply by looking at titles of books, the types of music, if the furniture is cheap, tacky, or designer. Are there plants? Pictures? Is it warm, lived in? Or is it cold, empty, sterile? A person who lives in a monastery with only one bag to her name is as telling as one who lives in a mansion crammed with material goods. (Also see Possessions above.)

In general, is she an indoor person? Does she hardly leave her house? Or does she love to be outside? Always feel confined, spend all day on her porch, hardly enter her house at all?

Geography: Location

What country is she in? What state? What town? What street? Where on the street? Does she have a view? What's the neighborhood like? Rich, poor? Dangerous, safe? Did she grow up there? Near there? (Living in her hometown is as telling as moving as far away as possible.) Is she a traveler? Is she near the ocean, mountains, forest, hills? What is the climate like? Why did she choose that location? Does she aspire for something different? What is keeping her there (family, job, friends)?

In general, would you consider her a city dweller? A nature lover? Is she a big traveler? Always on the road? Has she been to many countries around the world? Does she set sail for years at a time? Or has she never left her hometown?

Pets

Not every place will take pets, so this can be an important factor, as it often is in people's lives. Does she have a dog? What kind? (A rottweiler says as much as a poodle.) How many? For how long? Does she take good care of it? How big a role does it have in her life? (An owner who sleeps with the dog, cooks it gourmet meals three times a day, and takes it to therapy is as telling as one who kicks it when she feels like it.) Other pets? Cats? Fish? A snake? Hamsters? Rats? A talking bird? Any of these can say something about her. Does she yearn for a pet? Why can't she have it? Because of the building? Because she's allergic? Because her boyfriend is allergic? Does her pet annoy other people in her life? Does she get off on that?

Now apply these questions to the character(s) in your work. What details might you incorporate that you may not have thought of previously?

If you were to ask your character to analyze herself, would there be any discrepancies? Does she consider herself neat and tidy while her house is really in shambles? Does she consider herself the model neighbor while blasting her radio at 2 A.M.? Does she consider herself a devoted dog owner while only walking her dog once a week?

EXERCISE

From Outer Character Traits to Plot Points

The purpose of all those questions was to get you thinking about your character in a way you might not have before; if you were able to unearth even one new detail, it makes it all worth it. But there is another benefit to all those questions: Since this is a book on plot, we will now look at each of these character details and see how something as minor as a character trait can actually influence—in some cases, even define—the plot. By its end you'll begin to see that ideas for the plot can grow out of the characters themselves.

This is one of the more ambitious, time-consuming exercises of the book. For each character trait, ask yourself: How could this trait influence the plot? How could I base an entire story on this one trait? For instance:

Appearance: How could appearance influence the plot? Is she obese? (*What's Eating Gilbert Grape*) Deformed? (*Hunch-*

back of Notre Dame, My Left Foot) What about gender? Is she a woman battling to be accepted in a man's world? (*Shakespeare in Love*) Is he feminine? Is she masculine? (*GI Jane*) Or perhaps he/she is unsure about his/her gender itself? (*Boys Don't Cry, Flawless*)

Age: What events and dilemmas come with what ages? The six-year-old losing her teeth or dealing with the baby-sitters (*Home Alone*); the 12-year-old entering high school; the 13-year-old becoming bar mitzvahed; the 16-year-old celebrating her sweet sixteen (*Sixteen Candles*); the 18-year-old fretting about the prom or leaving for college; the 22-year-old being anxious about graduation and career; the 26-year-old facing pressure to marry; the 32-year-old carrying her first child; the 48-year-old having a midlife crisis; the 65-year-old having a retirement crisis; the 85-year-old dealing with a retirement home (*Cocoon*). . . . Any of these can make a story in and of itself—and you can play against the grain, too. What about the 40-year-old retiree? The 90-year-old worker? The child who graduates college at 19? The man who gets his degree at 41?

Medical Condition: How might a medical condition influence the plot? Has he caught a deadly virus? (*Outbreak*) Does a disease cut him down in his prime? (*Brian's Song*) Has he been told he has a finite amount of time to live? (*Blade Runner*) Or must he care for someone else who is dying? (*I Never Sang for My Father*)

Family: How might family dynamics influence the plot? Must she introduce her boyfriend to her parents? (*Meet the*

Parents) Must a girl marry according to the family tradition? (*Fiddler on the Roof*) Is a boy expected to take up his family's profession? (*The Godfather*) Must stepchildren learn to live together? (*Brady Bunch*)

Education: How might education influence the plot? Does a 40-year-old return to college to get his B.A.? (*Back to School*) Does a student spend a semester abroad? (*Oxford Blues*) Is he a teacher trying to hold a class together? (*Lean on Me*)

Employment: How might employment affect the plot? Is he finding his way in a new profession? Does it turn out that his company is crooked? (*The Firm*) Does she live for her job? (*Network*)

Police Record: How might a police record (or the obtaining of it) influence the plot? Did he commit his crime in an act of desperation? (*The Stranger*) Was he wrongly convicted? (*An Innocent Man*) Did he spend time in jail? (*Shawshank Redemption*) Did jail change his ways? (*American History X*)

Economics: How might his financial situation influence the plot? If poor, what would he do if he had a million dollars? If rich, how would he react if he lost it all? (*Trading Places*) Is his dire financial situation forcing him to take desperate measures? Rob a bank? (*Dog Day Afternoon*) A jewelry store? (*Straight Time*)

Romance: How might romantic relationships influence the plot? Does the ex-wife want to get back at her former husband? (*First Wives Club*) Is he attracted to younger girls?

(*Lolita*) Does she fall in love at first sight? (*Prelude to a Kiss*)
Is she a prostitute, trying to change her ways? (*Pretty Woman*)
Is he a bachelor with cold feet? (*My Best Friend's Wedding*)

Geography: Residence. How might his residence influence
the plot? (*Madame Bovary, Goodbye, Columbus*) Does he
live in a castle? (*Count Dracula*) Does she live in a haunted
house? (*Poltergeist*) Is he being held in a residence against his
will? (*Misery, Flowers in the Attic*) Does the action take place
in a hotel? (*The Shining*)

Geography: Location. How might location influence the
plot? (*Joy Luck Club*) Is the story heavily influenced by a suburban setting? (*American Beauty*) Does it play against the
grain of a normal suburban setting? (*Stepford Wives*) Is it a
remote, isolated landscape? (*Fargo, The Thing*) Or an over-
crowded urban environment? (*Soylent Green*)

Pets: How can a pet influence the plot? (*Walking and Talking*) Is the pet a savior, friend, protector? (*Lassie*) Or is it a
nuisance? (*There's Something About Mary*) A danger? (*Cujo*)
Or the viewpoint for an entire work? (*Cat's Eye*)

Possessions: How can possessions influence the plot? (*Shop
Girl*) Does the plot revolve around a piece of artwork? (*Mr.
Bean*) A jewel? (*Snatch*) Is the car all-important? (*Thelma and
Louise*)

Chapter Two

Characterization: The Inner Life

I would never write about someone who is not at the end of his rope.

—STANLEY ELKIN

A company can only ask a potential employee so much—if they probe into his sexual preferences or religious beliefs, they could get sued. If they probe deeper, into his superstitions or compulsions, they might be considered crazy. The public has made it clear that anything beyond a person's surface information must be kept private.

Paradoxically, when the public picks up a book, this is precisely the information they demand to know.

A writer, unlike a company, has no limitations. You have the depths of your character's psyche before you, and it is your job to plumb them. Unfortunately, many writers don't. Surface characterization, or the use of the characters merely as a vehicle for telling the story, is relied upon too often; in such cases, characterization often stops with little more than a basic, physical description, and the character's dialogue and actions will generally be convenient for the scene at hand.

Well-developed characters, by contrast, will have such a rich life of their own that you'll often find them thwarting your plans; once they are real, living people, they act like real, living people: whimsically and unpredictably.

This is where you enter the hazy territory of characters influencing—even defining—the story. If you keep an open mind and stay true to them, they will take over, scene after scene, and tell *you* how the action should be executed. This might mean throwing out much of your original plotting; it will certainly mean dropping your writer's ego; and none of it will be remotely possible unless you know, incontrovertibly, every aspect of your character's inner life.

According to astrology, our personalities are determined before we are born. What we are after in this chapter are not the superficial details of what this person does or where he lives or where he went to school, but *who he is*, a question rarely asked in society today. Let's consider the following:

Inherent Abilities: If someone is born with an innate ability (or disability) it can be a defining factor in his life—whether he spends his life embracing it or running from it, it will always be there. For Mozart or Michelangelo, their inherent abilities defined their lives. If one's IQ is 82 or 250, this is something that cannot be ignored; if one is psychic or dyslexic or color-blind or has an attention deficit disorder, this may have importance. Is he intelligent? Quick-witted? Or is he slow? Dull? Uncomprehending? Can he run with

Olympic speed? Throw a ball two-hundred yards? Does he have an incredible singing voice? Can he speed-read? Is he a contortionist? A master pianist? (*Shine*)

Religion: Although it often lurks beneath the surface in society today, mention a potential spouse and see how long it takes until your parents inquire about their religion. Walk the streets on Sunday mornings and you'll find most stores closed; enter a department store in December and you will be besieged by Christmas music. Whether we admit it or not, religion is a defining factor in our society and can be a defining factor in an individual's makeup.

In actuality, religion may play a huge part in a person's life, or no part at all. Either route is telling. Catholic? Jewish? Protestant? Muslim? Buddhist? Mormon? Hare Krishna? Is he observant? To what degree? Does he keep Sabbath? Shun pork? Does she wear a cross, attend daily confessional? Does he keep Ramadan? How big a role does religion play in his life? How observant is he in relation to the rest of his family? If he is observant but comes from a family that's not, it is telling; likewise if he is not observant but comes from a family that is. Is he out of touch with his religion? Would he like to know more? Is he on the verge of an awakening? Is she on the verge of turning her back on it? Does he live with religious guilt? How will he raise his kids? How does she want to raise hers? Is there conflict?

Spirituality: A person may be observant of his religion's rituals and yet deep down not believe in God. What is this person's relationship to God? Does he believe? If so, how strongly? How much thought has he given it? Have there been moments when, perhaps faced with death or great joy, he believed? Have there been moments when, faced with great evil or tragedy, he lost his belief? What triggered them, and what might trigger them again? Does he believe deeply in God, but not believe his religion's rituals? Or is he an atheist? Agnostic? Does he follow the latest New Age trends? Unfortunately, there is often a correlation between suffering and one's devoutness, especially if a person is coming to spirituality on his own. When did this person become religious? What triggered it? A death? Retirement?

Identity: At different points in our lives we play different roles. Parent, son, husband, student, employee . . . Ultimately these are all just roles, but often a person's very identity becomes wrapped up in them. People particularly tend to identify themselves with their career paths. For a policeman or a priest, a sense of identity might even be completely synonymous with the profession.

People often complain about their jobs, but when asked why they won't consider a new profession, they answer, "What else am I going to do?" They list a host of reasons that they can't risk trying anything else—wife, kids, house, mortgage, car payments—but often, deep down, it seems the other way around: A part of them has sought out these obligations so that they will no longer have to consider the possibility of a change. It takes great energy to consider many paths, and options can be paralyzing. After a point, whether the path is the best one is not as important as the fact that it is chosen. A certain sort of existential anxiety is abated, and one can proceed with confidence, channeling his energies toward one goal. This is the confidence of a man in his forties or fifties. What has he sacrificed for it?

Beliefs: A person's beliefs can be his defining characteristic—indeed, some will die for what they believe. Is he prejudiced? A skinhead? Does he attend KKK meetings? (Or is he a white man married to a black woman despite having been raised in a racist home?) Has he been indoctrinated by a cult? Has she chained herself to a tree to help save the rain forests? Does he bash gays on weekends?

The *source* of the beliefs are as important as the beliefs themselves. How many of his beliefs are the result of his own thought and how many the result of the influence of a parent, teacher, sibling, friend, movie, book, geography, economic status? Was he strong enough to resist these sources? At what age was he influenced by others? (For instance, Hitler did not become an anti-Semite until he was in his early twenties, when he was first subjected to widespread anti-Semitic literature and speakers.)

Programs: Programs are beliefs that lurk unconsciously beneath the surface, beliefs a person is unaware he has. For instance, he may have been raised during the Depression and as a result might go through life feeling as if money is scarce. Or he may have been raised by a parent who always told him he was stupid, and as a result might unconsciously feel that way. Or he may have experienced traumatic events that left deep, lasting impressions and cause him to relive the events for the rest of his life—like the abused child who attracts abusive partners in later life. What recurring themes or programs run through your character's life? Is he always short on money? Always in a volatile relationship?

Similarly, what is his sense of self-worth? Why doesn't he have all the money in the world, the CEO position, the beautiful girl, the huge house? Does he truly feel entitled to these things? If not, what programs are stopping him?

Ethics: How ethical is this person? Will he fudge a résumé? Inform a waitress if she left something off the check? Tell a cashier if she gave him a ten dollar bill instead of a single? Will he turn in a wallet he finds in a dark movie theater? Are his ethics dictated by the amount at hand? How principled is he, and what is his breaking point? If unethical, is he self-aware? Or, like most unethical people, does he use sophistry to convince himself that his actions are okay? Ethics (and their misuse) are at the core of many works—many plots revolve around finding a character's ethical breaking point. In works like *The Godfather,* Michael Corleone undergoes an ethical and moral odyssey, from abstaining from the family business to becoming enmeshed to the point where he would kill his own brother. His motives for entering the business are pure (to protect his father), but as he gets more involved he finds himself in an ethical dilemma (to protect his family or to murder others), and in one sense this work is about finding his ethical breaking point. In *Wall Street*, the son is drawn to increasingly greater power and fortune, but at the same rate his ethics are tested, to the point where he could destroy his own father's company for financial gain. *The Boiler Room* revolves around a similar theme.

Sex: In the previous chapter, we glanced at our character's surface romantic history—marriages, divorces, significant others, partners. As we probe deeper, into the part of the psyche that only we—as writers—can know about, we must know everything. What are this person's sexual preferences? Is she wild in bed? Is he unable to perform? Is he a virgin at thirty-five? Has she slept with five men by age fifteen? Is he a prude or does he believe in free love? When was your character's first sexual experience? Was it positive or negative? What has this person been raised to think about sex? Was it ever discussed? Was he raised by homosexual parents? Was he abused? What sort of partners has he attracted in the past? What does that say about him? How do his choices resemble his parents'? Does he have any sexually transmitted diseases? How has this affected his life? Does he want sex five times a day? Does she want sex once a month? Is she careful about protection? Is he careless? Is he into S&M? Does he frequent porn shops and peep shows? Will she refuse to even mention the word? What does this person look for in a mate? What type of ad would he place in the personals?

Motivation: What drives this person? What are his secret hopes? Dreams? Goals? What does he aspire to? What's in his way? Most of us live our lives trying to better whatever position we find ourselves in, instead of choosing a direction and pursuing it. For example, a college graduate lands a job at an advertising agency and, once immersed in that environment, can only focus on bettering his position within that company. How quickly he can lose sight of any greater goals, particularly if they weren't firm to begin with. Now is the chance to step back. What might his goals have been?

What motivates him? Money? Approval? Power? The fear of security? The need to provide for a family? Find a person's current obstacles, no matter how small, and you will likely find what he dwells on for most of his day. If the person is a child, he will likely dwell on his parents, the obstacles to freedom; if he is an employee, he will likely dwell on his boss or whatever obstacle lies in the way of his bettering his position. (The obstacle can also be abstract—for instance, the lack of a proper education.)

Friendships: For many, friends can be a defining factor in their lives. For instance, most cops and firemen will spend their free time with other cops and firemen; most military men will spend time with other military men. Who does he choose to spend time with? Coworkers, old college or high school buddies? What are his friends like? Are they crude, arrogant, insensitive? Are they a bad influence? Or are they successful, overachievers? Are they all celebrities? Are they all single at thirty-five? Are her friends all married at twenty? Are they all richer than her? Poorer? Prettier? Uglier? More educated? Less? What does that say about her?

Does he have few friends or many? Is he an introvert? A loner? Or is he an extrovert? Gregarious? Does he know everyone in town? Will he talk to everyone at a party?

Conversational Focus: You can learn a tremendous amount about people simply by observing what they choose to talk about. They might say they are merely rehashing the day's news when telling you a story about a local homicide, but the fact remains that they have chosen a morbid topic.

More tellingly, if you spend enough time with people, you'll find there is a recurring pattern to their conversational choices: They will often harp on the same themes, whether it is money, real estate, deaths, marriages, or child care; the funnies or the obituaries; the latest technology or the thirteenth century; fashion or fly fishing or the stock market. Conversation reflects what's on the mind. People do our jobs for us—they reveal themselves, if only we would listen. The problem is, we rarely listen carefully enough.

Self-awareness: Is he conscious of how others perceive him? Aware of his own shortcomings? His own strengths? Does he work to better himself? Does he see a psychiatrist, practice meditation, experiment with New Age methods? Can he admit he is wrong? Or does he live in a world of his own making, completely out of touch with reality? Does he see himself as beneficent while everyone else sees him as a monster? Does he consider himself brilliant and subtle, while everyone else sees him as stupid and obvious?

Values: What are the priorities in this person's life? God? Family? Work? Love? Power? Ethics? Erudition? If forced to choose between his wife and his work, which would he choose? If asked to do something unethical for his company, would he do it? Will he attend college at any cost? Will he leave his family to fight for his country?

Allocation of Time: Go through a weekday with him. A weekend. How does he spend his day? How much time is spent on what activities? How much of it is intellectual? Athletic? Mindless entertainment? Does he read Dostoyevsky in his free time or play Nintendo? Does he write poetry or frequent bars? Or both? Does he spend time with his kids or take care of his parents? Does he spend time with his girlfriend or spend time with his dog? Does he attend church twice a day or frequent sex shows? Or both? If he were to go on vacation, what would he do? Would he be restless, bored in two hours? Or would he be content to sit and read and think for days on end?

Artistic Impulse: The strength of one's artistic urge—and whether or not he has the ability, means, and forum to express that urge—is often of supreme importance. Hitler considered himself foremost an artist; what propelled him to his ultimate embitterment was his rejection from an art academy. If he had been accepted as an artist, the world might be different than it is today. For Nero, one of the greatest tyrants of all time, the fact that he was a world leader was less important to him than the fact that he was a singer, actor, and poet. Indeed, his final words were: "What an artist the world has lost."

Is your character an artist of some sort (painter, musician, writer, dancer, actor)? Does he do it on the side, or as a full-time job? If on the side, does he aspire to do it for a living? Has he tried to break through? What has he done? What instruments does he play? A guitar? Violin? The tuba? The drums? Is he any good? Does he play loudly in order to drive people crazy? Does he live in a happy home, but paint angry, dark faces? Is he a prig who nonetheless sculpts phallic symbols? What does this say about him?

If he exhibits nothing on the surface, is there repressed creativity in there somewhere? Is he a doctor penning a novel? A lawyer doing stand-up comedy? Is he a failed writer and thus a critic? A failed actor and now a casting agent?

Or has he never created anything in his life? Is he solely a laborer? Is he a pure businessman, banker, lawyer, doctor?

Heroes: When we are young, we have heroes. But as we age, as figures loom less large in our consciousness and we become more cynical about the creation of image, we are less quick to choose and maintain role models for ourselves. If forced, most of us will conveniently choose someone who is dead. Choose people who are alive. Who are your characters' heroes? If "hero" is too strong a word, think "role model"; if that is too strong, think someone they "look up to." We are all a mixed bag, and you might choose someone who is admirable in one area even if he is despicable in another. Do not expect all things from all people. They could be actors, musicians, humanitarians, politicians, soldiers, businessmen, mothers. . . . What does his choice (or refusal to choose) say about him? About what he values in life? What steps is your character taking to follow in the same path? Why or why not?

Politics and Ideology: Politics seem to sit in the background in America today, but if you bring up a political issue in a group of people, you'll find that nearly all have strong opinions, and nearly all differ. It is indeed rare to initiate a political discussion without walking away with a major argument and at least some venom. This is why many people will not discuss politics over a meal.

Is he Democrat? Republican? Independent? Liberal? Conservative? Anti-apartheid? For big tobacco? Is he pro death penalty? Pro gun? Is she anti-abortion?

Relationship to Authority: Is he a rigid authoritarian? Would he report you to the police if you ran a red light? Is he part of the establishment? Does he commute nine to five with the same group of people? Is he a member of a country club, on the board of several community committees? Or is he a rebel? An independent thinker? Will he refuse to hold a job, pay his bills? Is he always fighting the IRS, the Department of Motor Vehicles? How big of a part does his relationship to authority play in his life?

Vices: Vices can be incidental in a person's life, or they can be a defining factor. Is he a drug addict? An alcoholic? A chain-smoker? A chronic gambler? A sex addict? Has he ever tried drugs? Did it tarnish his record? Or, conversely, will he never drink? Can he not stand to be in a room where there is smoke?

Time Line: Most of us spend our time either reminiscing about the past or anticipating the future. Does your character spend most of his time reminiscing? Remembering old grudges? Thinking of an ex-partner? A deceased loved one? Regretting opportunities missed? Or is he always anticipating? Does he plan his life ten years in advance? Have a retirement fund set up at age twenty? Quietly bide his time, content to dream of a future promotion? Or does he live only for today? Refuse to think back, refuse to plan? You can also play against the grain. Is he a teenager who is always talking about his memories? An old man who is always thinking of the future?

Relationship to Food: A character's relationship to food can be a defining factor. Does he eat five times a day? Once a day? Does he gorge himself with massive amounts of food? Does he hardly eat at all? Is he obese? Anorexic? A vegetarian? A vegan? Strictly kosher? Is he addicted to caffeine? Chocolate? Is he lactose-intolerant? Allergic to white flour?

Are SpaghettiOs his idea of a good meal? Is caviar hers? Does he live on fast food? Does she insist on the nicest restaurants? Is his refrigerator always empty? Is her kitchen always full? Does he not know how to cook? Does she spend half the day over her stove? Are his table manners awful? Are hers priggish? How much time, energy, and money does this person devote to food? How big of a role does it play in her life? What steps must he take to conform his life to his eating habits? Live near kosher restaurants? Wake up at 5 A.M. to get in the first meal?

Habits: A professional hit man will watch his target. Within a few days, he'll find that his target sticks to nearly the same schedule every day—leaves the house at the same time, takes the same train . . . If he watches long enough, his job is done for him.

We are ultimately creatures of habit, especially as we get older. Does your character wake up at the same time every day? Go through his same morning routine—eat breakfast, read the paper, take the car, ride the train? Does he hang his shirts on the same side of the closet, tuck his shoes in the same corner? Does he frequent the same deli every day at 4 P.M. for his cup of coffee? Go to the same movie theater every Saturday night? Frequent the same hair salon the first Monday of every month? Vacation in the same place the last week of August every year? Is he a morning person, up every day at the crack of dawn? Or a night person, not awake until until 4 P.M.? Is he irascible in the mornings? Mindless at night?

Quirks: What peculiar quirks might this person have introduced into his life? Does he always need to carry an umbrella, just in case? Does he groom his dog every day? Does he feed the pigeons? Do irrational things set him off? People who are loud? Cigarette smoke? Does he hate the radio? Love LPs? Will he shun turtlenecks? Does she walk around nude?

Hobbies: Does he collect coins? Does she sew? Does he tinker with his car? Play poker every Thursday? Does she play bridge? Frequent flea markets? What sports does he play? Does he sail? Rock climb? Rollerblade? Go white-water rafting? Go to the gym? Does she play tennis? Swim? Play squash? Run three miles every morning? Is he a black belt in karate? Do they bowl as a couple? Which of these hobbies does he do alone? Which does she do with others? Who are their companions?

Charity: One can be generous and yet still not give to charity. For others, charitable work can be a defining aspect of their lives. How much of his money does he donate to charity? How much of his time? Does he volunteer for causes? Donate blood? Does he work for a nonprofit foundation? Join the Peace Corps?

Conversely, has he never given to charity, despite having

millions? Is he a celebrity who refuses to make even one charitable appearance? Has he been forced into giving to charity
or doing charitable work? Does he do it grudgingly? For
political reasons? Does he do it anonymously? Or with great
fanfare?

EXERCISES

• **The Personality Test.** Below find a list of positive and
negative character traits. For each trait, rate your character
on a scale of 1 to 10, on both the positive and negative side.
For instance, if your character is always generous and never
cheap, you would put a 10 in the generous column and a 0 in
the cheap column; if he is mostly generous but sometimes
cheap, you might put a 7 in the generous column and 3 in the
cheap column. People are a compendium of conflicting traits,
and a person can easily be generous in some areas but cheap
in others. When you have finished the test, tally up each side.
Overall, is the number higher on the positive or negative
side? By how much? Which traits are most pronounced?
What has this taught you about your character?

Negative	Positive
__Jealous? Covetous?	__Wish everyone the best?
__Cheap?	__Generous?
__Spiteful, vindictive?	__Forgiving?
__Stubborn?	__Pliable?
__Suspicious, paranoid?	__Trusting?
__Controlling?	__Easygoing?

Negative	Positive
__Dominating, a bully?	__Defender of the weak?
__Meek?	__Confident?
__Insecure, easily threatened?	__Secure?
__Low self-esteem?	__High self-esteem?
__Critical?	__Supportive?
__Competitive?	__Wants what's best for all?
__Makes fun of people?	__Praises others?
__An egoist, vain?	__Humble?
__Self-centered?	__Always thinking of others?
__Talks over people?	__A listener?
__Opinionated?	__Open-minded?
__Impractical?	__Practical?
__Unmotivated?	__Motivated?
__Unorganized?	__Organized?
__A follower?	__A leader?
__Directionless?	__Sense of direction?
__Undisciplined?	__Disciplined?
__Indulgent, wasteful?	__Conserver?
__Harsh, caustic?	__Kind?
__Impatient?	__Tolerant?
__Coward?	__Brave?
__Unproductive?	__Productive?
__Small goals?	__Ambitious?
__Afraid to take risks?	__Risk taker?
__Immature?	__Mature?
__Overly serious?	__Lighthearted?
__Morbid, a downer?	__Funny?
__Unhappy?	__Happy?
__Complainer?	__Content?

Negative	Positive
__Pessimist?	__Optimist?
__Worrier, uptight?	__Relaxed?
__Indifferent?	__Passionate?
__Overly emotional or excitable?	__Even-tempered?
__Temper?	__Calm?
__Violent?	__Peaceful?
__Argumentative, confrontational?	__Mediator?
__Shallow?	__Profound?
__Gossiper, slanderer?	__Speaks well of others?
__Cynic?	__Idealist?
__A talker?	__A doer?
__Manipulative, schemer?	__Straightforward?
__Liar, dishonest?	__Honest, principled?
__A taker, a user?	__A giver, a lender?
__Inconsiderate?	__Considerate?
__Terse, monosyllabic?	__Good communicator?
__Low energy? Drags you down?	__High energy? Filled with pep?
__Moody?	__Consistent?
__Defeating?	__Inspiring?
__Make others uneasy?	__Calming effect?
__Inspires guilt?	__Uplifts?

• **Friend and Family Profile.** Despite all of the questions in this chapter, none of this information will really hit home for you until you start working with it. It is easy to decide your character will, for instance, be greedy and suspicious. But that alone will not create him. It is just a small piece of the puzzle, and there remain thousands of other traits to consider. It can all seem overwhelming.

The best instructor is life itself. Start with the people closest to you. Go through your list of traits and ask yourself which apply to a particular friend or family member. Write them down and see if you have captured the person, if by simply listing his traits you can accurately depict a person to someone who has never met him. Probably not. Something mysterious remains to complete the picture. This is what makes people people. What is it? What's missing? Whatever it is, add it. Consider what you've learned by the omission and how it might apply when it comes time to build other characters.

• **Stranger profile.** Family and friends are easy. You know them. Now try meeting someone in a bar and setting them down on paper. You will have to form instant impressions, observe everything in a short period of time. Eventually, you won't have to go over your list of traits—instead, you'll find that a person's defining traits jump out at you.

Show your profile to five people and ask them their impressions of this character from your description. You'll be disappointed to find that all five have differing opinions, and probably associate him with someone else. Also notice that traits which had seemed so clear to you in the person's presence became hard to capture on the page, to articulate to others. Capturing and presenting a character in such a way that others can have an equally vivid experience of the person is an art in and of itself. Observing is only half the battle.

This is your training as a writer. You will improve on both fronts with practice.

• **Defining Characteristics.** Often when someone comes to mind, certain traits come instantly to mind with them. Consciously or not, you categorize this person. If you had to choose your character's three dominating characteristics, what would they be? This exercise will leave you with only the barest overview of your character; nevertheless, it is helpful—indeed, crucial—since it will tell you what first impression your character makes on others, and it is the first impression that often sticks. This will help you get an instant handle on him, and will be very helpful when you are dealing with many characters, especially when you need to keep in mind how many characters might interact with others (covered at length in Chapter Three).

• **Evolution.** You should by now have a pretty good sense of who this person is, but keep in mind that you only know who this person is *at this moment*. People change, day to day, year to year—indeed, the very point of most works is to show such a change. So, especially if there a passage of time, you will have to check in with your character at different points in your work and ask if all of this still applies. For instance, your character's goals will be different at sixteen than at twenty-eight. Has he outgrown his ambition? Has he changed hobbies? Has he become charitable? Consider these three exercises:

1) **Check in with his past.** Who was he twenty-years ago? Ten years ago? Five years? One year? Six months? Last

week? Was he a completely different person back then? Or has he remained exactly the same? (Both are telling.) How has he changed? Has he changed for the better or for the worse? For the better in some areas, for the worse in others? How does all of this affect who he is right now? For instance, say he is now a businessman, but ten years ago he was an actor—now you know he's not just an ordinary businessman, but one who perhaps still longs for involvement in the arts—or who perhaps has compensated by becoming hypercritical of them. Or say he's now a renowned food critic, but at one point in his life he was an Orthodox Jew. Taking his past identity into account, you now know that he's not just an ordinary food critic, but one who might feel guilt when he samples pork. How can all of this affect how you portray him on the page?

2) **The Catalysts.** Often it is specific events—not just the passage of time—that spark fundamental changes in a character. The death of a parent. The birth of a son. Marriage. Divorce. Jail. The new job. Reflect on who your character used to be and who he is now. When you think of how he is different, also think of what events may have occurred along the way to make him so. All of these catalysts hold tremendous potential for plot points. You can use them in flashback sequences, or extract them from his past and place them in the present. In either case, they are crucial to know, even if you don't use them, and can be used as rough stepping-stones along the path of a character's past.

3) **Check in with his future.** What are his plans for next week? Next month? Next year? His five-year plan? Where does he see himself in ten years? Twenty? Even if he is not

a planner, he still must have some vague vision of where he's heading. Is he a bachelor who'd like to marry and have kids? A prisoner who wants to go straight? A suburban man who wants more excitement? Is his focus only on material gain? Change of circumstance? Or is his focus on evolving as a person? Educating himself? Becoming more spiritual? Why does he want such a change? What does he hope to gain? How will his life change once he has it? What is he waiting for? What obstacles stand in his way? You now have a good handle not only on who he is, but on who he wants to become. This, inherently, will help create tension, since there is now a mission, a path. Even if he doesn't get what he wants, that, too, will be interesting, since we get to watch the difference between his imagined life and his real one, between anticipation and reality.

• **Identity.** How would your character respond to the question: "What do you do?" How closely intertwined will his answer be with how he sees himself as a person? How would your character respond to the more profound question: "Who are you?" Would he even be able to answer? How would this answer differ from his answer to, "What do you do?" Is there a discrepancy? How much of his identity is wrapped up in his career?

• **Outer and Inner Life Discrepancy.** As you conclude these first two chapters, you will have a good handle both on your character's outer and inner life. How big a discrepancy is there between the two? Or is there none at all? Does he put on a totally different face for the outside world? Or does he wear his entire life on his sleeve? Is his outer life misleading?

Is he an establishmentarian who secretly does drugs? The perfect husband who has affairs? The man with a long rap sheet who is secretly innocent and is, in fact, a great humanitarian? How will your character appear to others in the work? How does he act to his boss as opposed to his son, his friend, his wife? Is there a divergence in his behavior toward these different people? Might a teenager be relaxed and vulgar with his friends but somber and restrained with his parents? Might a father be easygoing with his wife but strict with his children? Which is the real him? Will other characters ever get past the veneer?

• **From Inner Character Traits to Plot Points.** This exercise is the same exercise that can be found at the end of Chapter One, except this one focuses on the character traits covered in Chapter Two—the character's inner life. Go through each topic covered—abilities, religion, spirituality, identity, beliefs, programs, ethics, sex, motivation, friendships, conversational focus, self-awareness, values, allocation of time, artistic impulse, heroes, politics and ideology, relationship to authority, vices, time line, relationship to food, habits, quirks, hobbies, charity, and personality—and ask yourself how any one of these characters traits might influence the plot. For instance, looking at the category of innate abilities, we might ask, does he have the innate ability of a master pianist? (*Amadeus*) Is she psychic? (*The Gift*) Is he slow? (*Sling Blade*)

• **The Unnameable.** The questions in these two chapters were crucial in that they got you thinking about aspects of your characters you may not have previously considered.

However, this is not to say that these questions are the final word, or that they can substitute for real life. They cannot. Real life is the best teacher.

I dislike the hackneyed phrase "Write what you know," since it implies you must "know" everything in order to write. That is not the case; some of the most famously realistic works were composed in complete isolation, by authors who had never set foot in the setting of their works and had no experience with the "real-life subject" of their work. Still, while you needn't necessarily "know" in order to write, it is often extraordinarily helpful to base your characters at least partially on real-life people. The point here isn't necessarily to capture reality but to aid your imagination by complementing it with real life—which is always a more complex, vivid, and unexpected tapestry than we could ever possibly imagine.

Having exhausted your lists of inner and outer character traits, go out and interact with people in real life. No matter how thorough you thought you'd been in advance, you'll find that some previously indistinguishable trait jumps out at you. What is it? Take it and run with it. *That* is your foundation. Like the electricity bolt that brings Frankenstein's monster to life, that is what will infuse life into your character.

Chapter Three

Applied Characterization

The moment comes when a character does or says something you hadn't thought about. At that moment he's alive and you leave it to him.

—GRAHAM GREENE

Plot does not magically appear with the creation of a character; Frankenstein's monster might open his eyes, but until he gets up from the table and *does* something, there is little basis for a plot. Plot comes with your characters taking action; with their interaction with others; with their traits being applied to imagined scenarios. At this point, if you've faithfully read and completed the exercises in Chapters One and Two, you'll have an excellent handle on your characters' inner and outer lives. This preparation was crucial, but unfortunately your task doesn't end there. On the contrary, it's just beginning. Now it's time to consider a whole new set of issues as you let your characters help you create your plot, as you begin to weave the endlessly rich and complicated tapestry of character inter-action.

Let us consider the following issues:

Major or Minor?

Will this be a major or minor character? Indeed, what is a major or minor character? Is it determined by the amount of space a character occupies in a work? Can't a character make a cameo and still be important—indeed, the most important? Couldn't one argue that Kurtz, even with his limited time on stage, is the major character in *Heart of Darkness*?

Many writers make the mistake of assuming that simply because they've given their character most of the stage time—usually in the form of the book's narrator or viewpoint charac-ter, or the screenplay's lead role—this suffices to make him the major character, and thus, ironically, less need be done to establish his centrality. This is why you'll sometimes walk away from a work remembering, ironically, not the "major" character, but a minor one. Characters with less space devoted to them are often better developed since the writer can take more time to craft them, to make the pages count, since they operate in such a small arena. It is for this same reason that the opening of a work is often better crafted than what follows: More thought, time, and energy are put into it because the writer deals with a smaller playing field. Once the field opens, and the writer sees the enormity of what's before him, he often, in a sudden panic of not being able to finish, lets down his guard and reduces his standards.

Go through your list of characters and ask yourself who

is major and who minor. Don't think in terms of space, but of importance. In your work, what will define major or minor? Although we meet him but once, is he the central influence? Although he's onstage throughout, is he really a foil for someone else? Are there several major characters? Is it an ensemble cast? Do they run parallel lives that in the end intertwine? Or separate lives, in separate acts, and never cross paths? The traditional single, sympathetic protagonist is still the strongest way to hold a work together. If you shy away from it, what will hold your work together in its stead? A common setting? An unusual time period? A common antagonist?

Frequency of Appearance

It is said that if one takes several short breaks when reading, the chances of comprehension are twice as great. This is because we tend to remember beginnings and endings much more than what comes between. Likewise, the frequency of a character's appearance can have an even greater impact than his time spent onstage. For instance, a character who fills sixty pages can appear only once (i.e., throughout the first sixty pages), or he might appear three times (e.g., in pages 1–20, in pages 200–220, and in pages 400–420). This technique is often used for effect in stalker works, where the stalker, although only onstage for a short time, appears frequently; the impact of all these appearances is a sense of ubiquitousness—it lends the stalker greater power and the victim a greater sense of futility or inescapability. How many appearances does your character make? Why this many? Can they be condensed to fewer appearances? Can they be stretched out to more?

Often it can feel suffocating if only one or two characters comprise the bulk of the work; we can easily get tired of them and want variety. Conversely, if a work switches among too many characters without devoting enough time to each, we can end up feeling as if we don't have an investment in any character. Or we can end up with just the right amount of time spent on various characters individually but feel as if they don't interact with each other enough, or don't all come together in the end, which can leave us feeling as if we've read a collection of disparate subplots. It is a delicate balance.

Entrances and Exits

Entrances and exits have power. In the famous shower scene in *Psycho,* what makes her murder shocking is not the actual stabbing but the fact that our protagonist, unexpectedly, is yanked offstage early in the film. The antagonists in *Silence of the Lambs* and in Flannery O'Connor's "A Good Man Is Hard to Find" gain their frightening power by not making their appearances until the very end. Conversely, in *The Dinner Game* a character who should exit in the first act lingers on; it becomes the gimmick of the film and lends it humor. When does your character first appear? On page 1? Page 50? The very end? What would happen if he appeared later? Earlier? Conversely, when does he exit? What would happen if he exited earlier? Later?

Perception and Reaction

Two men stand in line at a bank at 2:50 P.M.

The first, anticipating long lines before closing, has brought a book to read, and waits contentedly. He looks up from time to time, sees the tellers are working as hard as they can, sees that they are at the end of a long day, and feels sympathy for them. He thinks of how, when it's his turn, he'll apologize for keeping them late, compliment them on their work, and show his gratitude before leaving.

The second man, needing to be somewhere else by 3:00 P.M., stands on line fidgeting, fuming, and complaining to anyone he can find. He glares at the tellers. He sees them as privileged, getting to sit comfortably under air-conditioning in the awful heat and call it a day by 3 P.M. He sees them as lazy, stupid, too incompetent to count money efficiently and hasten their customers off the line—in fact, he's sure that they are deliberately stretching out their customers so as to not have to deal with as many people, and perhaps even to shut down the bank before he personally can get his turn. He catches one looking back at him and becomes positive they are taking their time just to spite him. Knowing he is being publicly made a fool of, he is now indignant, furious. He thinks of how he'll chastise them when it's his turn, really let them have it before he leaves.

In actuality, these two men are in the exact same circumstance. It is their *perceptions of* and *reactions to* the circumstance that differ.

As human beings, we constantly gauge others to see how they perceive and react to events—so that we can better know ourselves. If you are the only person in a movie theater of 500 who's not scared, you might walk out of that theater concluding that, based on others' reactions, you are a person not easily scared. If all the characters in your work throw a surprise birthday party for your protagonist and he opens the door and curses them all, what is the telling factor? The party? Or the character's reaction? What has this taught us about him?

Ultimately, events and circumstance are not half as important as how characters perceive and react to them. Before you put your character into your story (where events and other characters are constantly changing), you must first get a handle on how he might perceive and react to the world around him. You must keep this in mind constantly as you go. For instance, characters can perceive themselves as acting one way when in fact they are acting another. It is not uncommon for people to feel as if they are acting kindly while treating other people harshly. The abusive boss or abusive spouse will not consider himself abusive, for if he did he wouldn't be able to live with himself; or, he might have a glimmer of his own abusiveness but might justify it to himself (e.g. the worker deserved it). Indeed, a discrepancy between a character's interior monologue and his actions is a powerful tool to show a character out of touch with himself.

A character's perception becomes a thousand times more relevant—can indeed define the entire work—if he happens to be the narrator or viewpoint character.

Narration

Who should narrate (or be your viewpoint character)? A major character? A minor one? A few characters? What difference does it make? How will it impact the work as a whole?

Choosing a narrator or viewpoint character is not a choice to be made lightly, yet unfortunately many writers make the choice without giving it much thought. Generally, they automatically assign the task to the protagonist. There is nothing necessarily wrong with this choice—in fact, most often, it is the correct one—but problems can arise if the decision was made without taking the time to consider why this person has merit as a narrator, what perspective he has to offer, what he brings to (or how he detracts from) the telling of the story, and how his perspective might differ from others'. This issue is also relevant for the screenwriter (who doesn't employ a narrator but who does choose a viewpoint character) and for those who choose multiple narrators or viewpoint characters. (For our purposes, we exclude omniscient and framed narration.)

Many writers make the mistake of thinking a narrator's (or viewpoint character's) only objective is to tell the story. In fact, the narrator has three objectives:

1) **The first objective is, indeed, to tell the story, to describe the unfolding of events.** On a basic level, the reader needs to know what's happening. To fulfill this task, you'll need a narrator who is lucid, a good observer, accurate with facts and details, and can present information in a simple, straightforward manner. He is like a cameraman: If the camera is jolted, or

out of focus, one cannot follow what's going on. Thus, it can be very dangerous to tinker with your narrator's basic storytelling abilities.

However, these *can* be tinkered with—something that many writers don't consider. For instance, is your narrator insane? Does he get facts plain wrong? Or is he a liar? Does he describe events that do not happen? Does he filter events to suit his needs? Then how can we, as readers, know what is accurate and what is simply his version? How can we get the story straight?

It is easy to see how difficult such a work could be on the audience—most readers would get fed up and set it down. If you were to employ an unreliable narrator, either the narrator would have to be unreliable only in doses (say, he is temporarily under the influence of drugs), or he would have to be contrasted with other narrators who were reliable, giving us a beacon for the actual story. We can tolerate an out-of-focus camera temporarily, if done for the right reasons, but few viewers can sit through an entire film that way.

2) **The narrator's (or viewpoint character's) second mission is to color the story with his perspective.** This must be done for two reasons: (i) without a perspective, the telling of a story can become flat and dull. Having a perspective on events—any perspective—gives us a vested interest in the character and the story. Without it, the work can feel like detached summary; and (ii) there is no better way to learn about a character than to observe his perspective—and since the narrator (or viewpoint character) is, ostensibly, one of the most important characters in the work, he is an

important person to learn about. And since there is no one else telling the story (except in the case of multiple narrators), our narrator's perspective is our chief way to learn about him (unless he himself were to stop the story and say, "Let me tell you about me," which, obviously, is not preferred).

For instance, let's take our two characters on line at the bank and say we had to choose one of them to narrate. How might the choice impact the story? The first man would likely give us a more balanced perspective of what was happening—probably also a very boring one. The second man's perspective would be filled with rage and paranoia—but it would be interesting. It might even create suspense where there was none; then again, it could be overwhelming for an entire work.

In either case, this change of perspective would change our entire experience of it. Whose version is the right one? Both. Each has his own, equally valid, take on reality. The tellers' kindness is a reality for the first; the tellers' spitefulness is a reality for the second. In actuality, are the tellers kind or spiteful? Or neither? Who is in the position to make that judgment? Ultimately, as writer you must ask, what is the objective of the work, and which viewpoint will best serve it overall?

A narrator's perspective can be the single defining factor of a book. As we grow to trust our narrator (as we will in most cases), we unconsciously take on his feelings and views. If he loves a certain person, so will we; if he hates him, so will we. Indeed, it becomes nearly impossible for us to form detached opinions of others in the work when all is filtered through one narrator. In some rare cases, we will dislike or distrust our narrator; in such works the narrator's perspective is still a defining factor, though, since we form our impressions of what to like based upon what he does *not* like.

It isn't always so simple as a narrator outright telling us what he does or does not like. Indeed, such a narrator might come off as opinionated and dominating and might turn off a reader, since nobody likes being told what they should think of someone; on the contrary, readers like to be able to form opinions for themselves. Outright telling them how they should feel about certain characters is a mistake many beginning writers make. More experienced writers filter a narrator's perspective through his *choice* of observations. Observations *are* a choice.

For instance, let's say a man walks into a room wearing a thousand-dollar suit, but his hair is not perfectly combed. Our narrator might mention only the hair. He is not giving us his opinion; he is merely stating the facts. But he is choosing *which* facts to state. In this subtle way, he is hinting at what impression we should form of this man. A more subtle narrator will mention both the suit and the hair, but will mention the suit in passing and spend more time on the hair. Technically, he has described both. But he has emphasized the latter.

Indeed, a narrator's perspective can create a guessing game. Is this what is really happening, or is it just our narrator's biased perspective? Take our paranoid narrator at the bank. If he tells us the tellers are looking at him spitefully, why should we not believe him? If it is later in the work, we might know better, but if we haven't spent a great deal of time with him—say it is the opening scene—we have no way of knowing. When will we find out that the tellers are, indeed, not spiteful, and that we are just experiencing our narrator's biased perspective? After two, three, four incidents like this? Halfway through the work? Not until the end? Or never? Will it always be a mystery, open for debate? Will the reader want to go back and read the work again? "Reality" can get distorted very quickly, and this guessing game can be a source of satisfaction for the reader.

Perspective is delicate, though, and if not handled properly, can cause grievous problems. It can be overdone, something many beginning writers do. In such cases, the work becomes all about the narrator and less about the story; it can be suffocating. One quickly loses sight of the story, and readers will resent you for it and put it down.

Once beginning writers stumble upon the power of perspective—learn that it can be more influential than actual events—they often develop a sort of euphoria and decide to go overboard. This is typically and unfortunately the motivating factor behind the use of multiple narrators and points of view, which is why I discourage it. Multiple narrators or viewpoints are almost always employed at the expense of the basic telling of the story. In such works you'll often find repetition, necessary in order to give us the back story of a new perspective; the problem is, the story itself no longer moves forward. Few works can switch narrators frequently and still unfold a story with fluidity, partly because the learning of the viewpoint itself takes an effort for the reader and must, by nature, slow down the telling. It is in fact rare to encounter a work which genuinely needs multiple narrators and genuinely uses them for maximum effect. (This is not to say it is impossible. Some works, like Faulkner's *The Sound and the Fury*, do pull it off brilliantly, and indeed it is this very alternating of viewpoints that lends them their richness.)

The narrator's (or viewpoint character's) first and second objectives conflict with each other. The objective to tell a story with impartiality conflicts with the objective to color it with perspective. The best writers can achieve both objectives, with each enriching the other. But achieving a balance between the two is one of the most difficult things to achieve in writing. In every sentence lies an opportunity to reveal something about the narrator. This opportunity should not be lost; then again, it should not be taken advantage of.

As if all of this were not enough, there is a third objective for the narrator:

3) **The narrator's (or viewpoint character's) third mission is to convey his personal involvement in the story.** The viewpoint character must be in every scene (especially in the form of a novel); otherwise, how could he describe events? Having one person in every scene can be overwhelming; like living with someone, we might occasionally want a break from him. (This is why I might (rarely) recommend a switch in viewpoint characters, if done using third-person limited narration, only at a chapter or section break, and in a way which gives different viewpoints equal weight

in the work. This is another problem with first-person narration: Switching viewpoints is not an option. The *only* way the narrator can tell the story is to be in every scene—either that, or to have the story told to him secondhand, which is often awkward.) If our viewpoint character is also the center of attention, and the focal point for dialogue and circumstance, it can be like one person writing, directing, and starring in a movie.

The pull for attention from these three objectives becomes most apparent when we consider how they might conflict with each other. For instance, our viewpoint character's actions might contradict his perspective. Let us suppose he has been telling us throughout the work how much he hates Character A, and yet as soon as Character A enters the scene, he says to him, "I admire you so much." If we assume that our viewpoint character has been telling us, as readers, the truth (which we always will), then we must wonder why he is thinking one thing and saying another. Is he too spineless to tell people how he really feels? Is he on the spot, caught in a moment of nervousness? Is he the type of person who can't control what he says? Has he had a sudden change of heart he hasn't yet told us about? Or is Character A his boss, and is he just being politic? Did he hint earlier that he would act against his perspective, or was it a surprise to us? If so, why did he keep us in the dark? What have we learned about him as a result? Can we still trust him?

A viewpoint character might not get personally involved in events at all; for instance, a boy sitting in the rafters and reporting on the adults' behavior below. What do we gain by witnessing the scene from the rafters? What do we lose? Let's go back to our men at the bank. What if the viewpoint character of that scene was not Man 1 or Man 2, but a bored, impartial clerk, watching this events unfold from his desk? We would gain distance and more objectivity. There is a better chance that this clerk is telling the truth, since he is not intimately involved with the events and doesn't really care about them. But we would lose personal involvement, immediacy, and tension. We are suddenly not on anyone's side. Who cares what happens? Why watch the scene at all?

Ultimately, you must ask yourself whose story is this? Can I best bring this person to life through his viewpoint, or by using someone else's? Is the wife in the best position to tell her husband's story? Is the psychiatrist in the best position to tell his patient's?

Through Others' Eyes

In the opening scene of *The Godfather*, the character of Don Corleone is established without his doing or saying a thing. He sits behind a master desk, in a room of quietly devoted supporters, while across from him a man pleads for help and forgiveness. We know who Don Corleone is simply by watching *the way others treat him*.

Conversely, in *Revenge of the Nerds*, the college ensemble shows us how the nerds are thought of. Yet, despite this, we grow to like and sympathize with the nerds; moreover, we grow to dislike the ensemble that treats them like nerds and to learn that it is the people casting the stigma—not the stigmatized—whom we should dislike. This principle—how others are thought of—is the crux of the film (used, in this case, for comic effect). In most cases, though, the endearing of a stigmatized character is used for dramatic, even tragic effect, such as in *Sling Blade*.

Sadly enough, consciously or not we often look to see how people are treated by others to take our cue on how we should treat them. If we enter a room where everyone is bowing to a king, we will probably do the same; if we enter a town where people are keeping their distance from a mumbling village idiot, we will probably do the same. This is what can make for a "mob mentality," where, if caught up in an angry, impassioned mob, you will likely allow yourself to become caught up in their cause, even if you are barely sure what it is.

This insidious human trait can rear its head in much less extreme, everyday situations, and often does: Let's say it is your first day in a new school or office, and you observe everyone avoiding or mocking a certain person; you, likely, will avoid him, too, if for no other reason than not to be associated with him. Conversely, you will also take cues on whom to respect, and might look to become closer to such a person, if for no other reason than that others might then respect you, too. When you are more comfortable, and have been in the new environment for a while, you might take a step back from the mass consciousness and make decisions for yourself—even if they go against the grain—and decide the universal weirdo is not weird after all, and perhaps even befriend him. But on that first day, overwhelmed with people to meet, you make instant decisions, as the only possible way to make distinctions. You are vulnerable to the perceptions of the masses.

The same holds true for your readers, who are introduced all at once to an entire cast of characters. They need to make decisions, and they look to take cues. Lesser writers might shove these cues down readers' throats, outright tell them what opinions to form. Better writers will introduce us to a new character by dramatizing how others act toward him. Show B, C, and D taunting A in the schoolyard. Show B, C, and D coming to A for advice. Show B, C, and D asking A for protection. This is one preferred method, since it allows readers to come to their own conclusions, and also leaves room for interpretation and ambiguity.

The way a character is treated by others is an opportunity to teach us not just about our character, but also about the people doing the treating—indeed, sometimes this is the very point. If characters A, B, and C surround character D in the schoolyard, the point might be to show that D is the type that gets picked on—or it might be to show that A, B, and C are bullies.

Consider the following:

• How do the other characters treat your viewpoint character? What specific actions do they take against (or with) him? What do they say to him? What do they say to others about him in his presence? What does he hear, secondhand, they are saying about him behind his back? What can this teach us about him?

• How does your viewpoint character perceive others' treatment of him? Is he like our man in the bank who perceives hostile action toward him when there is none? Or is she an abused spouse, who describes her husband striking her but perceives nothing wrong with the action? What does this discrepancy between perception and reality teach us about her?

• How does your viewpoint character treat other characters? One of the best ways to gauge how your character treats others is to see how he reacts when he is given an objective which is of no importance to him but of great importance to someone else. Take, for example, a courier charged with delivering a package of blood for a dying man. What if the courier knows what's inside but decides to empty it on the street? Then we might label him evil. What if he does so because the recipient of the package wronged him a long time ago? Then we might label him vengeful. What if he intends to deliver it but is just taking his time, not caring when he arrives? Then we might label him either selfish and cruel, or perhaps psychotic, out of touch with reality. Conversely, what if the package is only a piece of candy for a sick boy, and he rushes through the streets—putting his life at risk—to get it there as soon as he can? Then we might label him saintly. As we can see, the way someone handles an objective of importance to others can go a long way in giving us insight into the character himself.

• How do the other characters treat each other? How does the viewpoint character perceive they treat each other?

• How would your viewpoint character react if someone treated him differently than he anticipated? What would Man 2 in the bank do if the tellers were nice to him? What would Man 1 do if they were mean? Will this change their perception? Or confirm it? Will it make us trust their judgment less? More?

Group Characterization

Have you ever been part of a group where the collective chemistry was unmistakable? Three best friends? A soccer team? An acting class? A committee? Where, despite coming together for a short time, the group stayed friends for years? Or, conversely, where the tension was unmistakable? Where you could not have put more badly matched people together in a room? Where the fighting never stopped?

In Chapters One and Two, you learned to create the individual character. Now it's time to see if the characters you've created were good choices collectively, if your cast has the potential for strong interaction. If you make good choices, you'll know right away, and the pages will come alive. Think of *The Breakfast Club*, or *The Odd Couple*. Character interaction propelled these works.

If you put a general and a draft dodger in a room, the scene will create itself. If they are genuine characters (not types), then maybe the results will even be unexpected. Maybe the general had once tried to dodge the draft but was forced into the military by his family. Maybe the draft dodger wanted to join but was cajoled into hiding by his girlfriend.

Maybe they are both diehard patriots, but have different ways of expressing it. Maybe they have a lot in common. Maybe they both collect coins, are experts in astronomy. (See Chapter Six: Conflict.)

Conversely, if your collective choices are bad, you'll often know it right away, too. The scene will feel flat, no matter what you do. You'll find yourself working ten times as hard to make it come alive—you'll try to make the dialogue more witty, the setting more unusual, you might add a suspenseful element, even try to spice up the characters themselves—but these are all just surface remedies for a scene that was lost before you began. Often, as editor, I must work on a book that is already bought, or one that a writer is already set on; the setup won't be changed, so I must salvage what I can. I might help add all of these elements, make it livelier, more readable, more engaging—but fundamentally it will never be a great work, since the choices were wrong to begin with. It is like having one hand tied behind my back.

Instead of merely salvaging, let us first strive for the great work. Look at your cast of characters. Are there any people who are diametric opposites? Extraordinarily similar? Do any have common ground? Something that binds them? Are they working together toward a common goal? (Do they hate each other despite that?) Do they have something that drives them apart? Conflicting agendas? Are they of different classes, different races? Incompatible astrological signs? (Do they love each other despite that?)

Similarities or differences needn't be major to cause a major difference of opinion. For instance, A and B might get along fabulously except for the fact that A might hate smoke and B might be a chain-smoker; or A might hate loud people and B might have a booming voice. (See Chapter Six: Conflict.) Such minor, seemingly insignificant details can dictate an otherwise thriving relationship. This is the beauty of putting characters in a situation where they are forced to be with each other. Each must learn tolerance and compromise; each must learn about himself and others; and each, if he can get past his petty annoyances (or superficial preferences), might come to see there is much more in the other than he had thought.

Time Spent with Each Other

How much time do your characters spend with each other? Do many characters interact in every scene? Or are there ten isolated characters in ten different scenes, with no one interacting with anyone? Characters needn't necessarily interact with each other, but the less character interaction there is, the more you'll need to make up for it in other ways. You might, for instance, link them by an unusual time, concept, or setting; even in such cases, though, one could argue that the added element is a character in its own right. In *The Shining*, for instance, the hotel is as much—if not more—of a character than the people; although, as the work progresses, the characters interact less and less, the hotel serves to bind them, playing an increasingly greater role.

Consider, as well, the *type* of time characters spend with each other. Is the work rife with cursory meetings, with people meeting each other in passing, at a bus stop, a bar, never really getting to know one another? Or do the characters get to know each other intimately, share a prison cell for ten years, go through an ordeal together? Can a character truly get to know someone despite a fleeting encounter? Or can he never really know someone, despite living with him his whole life? Ultimately, we come to learn that knowing another person is not about the sheer amount of time spent with him, but about the quality of that time, a character's willingness to learn about another, and another's willingness to share of himself.

Consider, as well, if the characters *want* to spend time with each other. The concept of two characters who want to get away from each other but can't is a powerful enough tool to propel an entire work (*Midnight Run*). What obstacles lie in the path of their getting away from each other? Have they both been assigned to the same army barracks? Assigned the same dorm room? Are they teammates? Cellmates? Conversely, the idea of two characters who want to be together but can't is an equally powerful tool. What obstacles lie in the path of their coming together? Powerful families? (*Romeo and Juliet*) Gaps in geography? Money? Age? Or, perhaps Character A wants to spend time with Character B, but Character B wants to get away? Is Character A a stalker? An aggressive suitor? A hanger-on?

Group Behavior

A group of people can be considered a character in its own right, and its presence can be powerful enough to help sustain an entire work. Think of a gang (*The Warriors*); a company (*Network*); a family (*Ordinary People*). Something magical happens when people come together as a unit; groups simply behave differently than individuals.

If your character is part of a group, how might its dynamic affect him? Does he get caught up in it? Does he act differently as a result of its indoctrination? Is he now a devout Hare Krishna? A brazen corporate salesman? An army disciplinarian? A street gangster? Does he only act differently in the group's presence? Or has he been changed permanently? Or is he immune to the group altogether? Has he, on the contrary, influenced the group? Has he single-handedly defied it? (*On the Waterfront*) Got it to change its ways? Individuals and groups can be used as markers against each other; there is no better way to help define each. You can also pit an unaffiliated individual against an outside group (*Invasion of the Body Snatchers*), just as you can pit one group against another group.

It is possible to create a world through a burst of genius, through an elaborate and clever setup of time and place and pure concept—like, say, *Blade Runner*—but you can also, more easily and consistently, create a world with a mere group of people. *The Godfather* worked on both levels, creating an original world of time, place, and concept and yet maintaining strong group (in this case, family) dynamics; we admire the movie as much for teaching us about the Mafia as we do when Tom tells Michael that he always wanted to be considered a brother to him. (This is why the ending of *Godfather II* is so shocking—the Mafia concept intertwines with Michael's killing of his own brother, and we realize the two dynamics cannot coexist.) *Star Wars* did the same, creating an utterly exotic world of time and place and creatures while maintaining group dynamics not only with opposing groups and armies, but even on the most intimate level, with basic family dynamics. Indeed, the family dynamics in *Star Wars*, with its melodrama and hidden secrets, nearly borders on soap opera-ish; it might, if transplanted, work on an episode of *One Life to Live*. But this is exactly what is needed to counterbalance the utter foreignness of the world. It is not by accident that both of these works were among the greatest blockbusters of all time—and also spawned many sequels.

Circumstance

Character A is a diehard patriot. He believes and has always espoused that one should kill for one's country. His country is at war, he has been drafted, and he sits in a trench with his gun aimed at the enemy. He has him in his sights. But, after a tense moment, he cannot pull the trigger.

Character B is considered the coward and weak link of the platoon. A small, frail man, he is opposed to killing, can hardly handle his weapon, has always acknowledged that he is unfit to be a soldier, and exudes none of the machismo or tough talk of his fellow soldiers. Yet one day a live grenade is thrown into a room and he, without hesitating, jumps on it, sacrificing himself while the ten other soldiers sit frozen in fear.

A character can think and feel one way, yet when the time comes to act, behave very differently. It is only through *circumstance* that we get to see our character in action, get to know what he is really made of. As a writer, it is your job to create that circumstance. If the circumstances are strong enough, your characters will act and react naturally, and will come alive as a result. They will tell you, by their actions, who they are. If you create the right circumstances, you will find scene after scene unfolding by itself, and in the process will learn more about your character than you ever could have otherwise.

Without circumstance to prove a character's mettle, it can be hard to gain perspective and make a judgment about him. This especially holds true with respect to our viewpoint character. The experience of being in one character's head throughout an entire work can be deceptive. Eventually, it becomes hard *not* to sympathize, just by virtue of spending time with him, by being let into his secret thoughts; his hopes become our hopes. We become so caught up in the character's internal dialogue that we forget to take a step back and judge him by his actions.

But when we finish the work and reflect on it, when we recap it to ourselves (or others), it is the character's actions we must recall, not his thoughts (however villainous or charitable), since the character's actions are the action of the work, and are the only concrete events we can point to. If a character thinks loving thoughts for two hundred pages then shoots his friend, and someone asks us what the work was about, we are not going to answer, "It is about someone who thinks loving thoughts," but will answer, "It is about someone who shoots his friend." If you look at your characters' thoughts and actions in relation to each other, often you'll be surprised to find there is a discrepancy (just as in real life there can be a discrepancy between our own thoughts and actions).

One must be careful, though, about labeling a character permanently based on one circumstance. Take an eighteen-year-old soldier who's afraid to pull the trigger. Meeting that person at that moment in time, you might conclude that he's not the sort of person you could depend on if your life were on the line. However, at age twenty the same soldier might be the disciplined killer of his platoon. Such discrepancies in a character's reaction to circumstance can be a powerful tool in helping create his arc and journey. (See Chapter Four: The Journey.) Has he used a circumstance as a learning experience, as an opportunity to grow and change? Has a circumstance traumatized him?

Even if a character does not change, his inability to act does not necessarily negate his beliefs. Character A might be a diehard patriot and might incite others to kill, but might be unable to do it himself. One could label this hypocrisy, but that would be too simplistic. There exists a magic gap between talk and action, and inaction doesn't necessarily negate beliefs. However, at the end of the day, regardless of beliefs, a character must be judged based on his actions.

As extremes in temperature are needed to test a bowl's breaking point, so can extreme circumstances bring out in a character what we might never know otherwise. We gain a new respect for the man who can stoically bear sadistic torture, as we gain a new loathing for the man who gives up all of his comrades before the torturer even begins to threaten. If it weren't for the Russian roulette scenes in *The Deer Hunter,* we'd have an entirely different relationship to the characters (as they would to each other). And yet circumstances needn't always be extreme. Torture is far from everyday life, and if you rely on it (or some equivalent) to teach us about your characters, you might find your work filled with extravagant circumstances few can relate to. Consider the following circumstantial elements:

Suffering. Suffering can bring out a lot in a person. How does he react to the death of a parent? Does he sob for months? Or not shed a tear? How does he react when diagnosed with cancer? Faced with bankruptcy? Publicly defamed? How about when faced with something more mundane, like having to work for an ungrateful boss? Or having a persistent toothache? Does he become grouchy? Lash out at others? Has he suffered all his life and remained stoic in the face of it? Or can he not handle it at all? Will he do anything to avoid pain?

Sacrifice. It is rare to be faced with the dilemma to kill or be killed. More often, sacrifice comes in smaller, less obvious ways. Does he give up his seat on the subway? Work quietly to support his parents? Stay in on weekends to watch his sister's kids? Is he always looking to be a martyr? Or will he never do anything for anyone but himself?

Environment. There is truth in the adage that you learn a lot about a person by traveling with him. Simply changing a character's environment can reveal much about him. How might a city person react in the jungle? (*Romancing the Stone*) A country person react in Manhattan? (*Midnight Cowboy*) How would a rich person act in a trailer park? A trailer park kid act in a Park Avenue mansion? Does he hate the cold? Come alive in the heat? Is he adaptable to whatever environment he's in? Or does he hardly change regardless of where he goes?

Difficult Moments. Consider what this character's weak spots are, what buttons you can push. Take a man who is always civil, make him skip breakfast, lunch, and dinner, put him on a crowded commuting train at rush hour, give him an aching foot, make him stand, and make the train stop in the tunnel and not move for an hour. Then have someone step on his foot. Will he snap? Seemingly petty circumstances can change people for brief moments. Whether or not these changes are a reflection of their character depends on how frequently and easily they react to such moments, and whether their reaction is disproportionate to the circumstances. It is natural for a person to snap at such a moment; however, if he did not snap, if he remained stoic and patient, this would tell us much about him; conversely, if he snapped after three seconds of waiting (instead of one hour), this would also tell us much about him. But we can't learn anything without the circumstance, so it is up to you to create it.

Multidimensionality

There's a difference between a character having moments—doing something temporarily out of character as a result of circumstance—and a character being multidimensional. Take the case of a kind man who is agitated and snaps at a child. The character who's merely having a moment will regret his action; the multidimensional character, on the other hand, will not see anything wrong with his action, and might even do it regularly.

Characters, being human beings, can act paradoxically. A man who devotes his life to charity might also beat his wife; a woman who devotes her life to rescuing children might scream at her own. Take the man who won't speak under torture. Let's say that until that point he has been an utterly annoying, cowardly person—a character we have despised.

Now we have reason to like him. Which stance do we take? Being human beings, we like to make decisions about people, to know how we should feel about them. We like to weigh their faults against their virtues—not to itemize and hold distinct each and every one—and make a blanket decision. In this case, if we were to weigh the virtues against the faults, his faults would still win. Probably we would still hate him, although with some reservation.

One of the chief functions of multidimensionality is to make a work more realistic, to make it easier for us to relate to the person. It is hard for us to relate to the perfect man. But throw a few faults in, and he becomes more like us. It is hard for us to see ourselves as Superman, but we can almost see ourselves in the shoes of a Serpico. We all have some areas where we are heroes and some where we are cowards; showing all sides of a character is what helps makes him real. Making a character morally complex also adds richness to a story, leaves room for us to argue who's right and who's wrong; it lends a certain kind of philosophical fulfillment we would be hard-pressed to find in a one-dimensional *Batman and Robin*.

Multidimensionality, though, can be difficult to achieve and can be a major problem if not done in expert hands. The more layered a character is, the harder it is to decide if we like him, if we should be on his side. Many writers end up creating characters who are not clearly sympathetic or unsympathetic—instead, they are just mundane and uninteresting. This creation of "morally ambiguous" characters can be a convenient excuse for writers who are undecided, who lack the boldness to commit to certain characters, or, most commonly, who shoot for "realism" at any cost.

"Reality" has become the shrine in today's culture—"reality" programming (TV shows like *Real World* and *Cops*), reality films (*Blair Witch Project*), 24/7 live cams where you can watch on the Internet everything that is "really" happening today. . . . It was reported that in 2001, approximately 70 percent of the new television programming was going to be reality-based. We can hardly blame writers for striving for realism, since they are pounded with the cliché "write what you know" as a mantra in all writing workshops. Realism has its advantages: It can make a work more plausible, allow suspension of disbelief to occur more easily (since very little is needed), and make the work more relatable. The effect, though, of valuing realism above all else is that we are often left with no one to root for, or actively despise. It strips all heroes and ideals away. It makes the very idea of a hero repugnant, since that would be far from "reality." One notices the difference even in films of the last twenty years: It doesn't feel as if a *Rocky* or *Conan*—a work featuring an unabashedly, morally uncomplex hero—could be made today. As a result, we are left with few genuine heroes, few role models—only the everyday reality of everyone else's lives. Art has become less an escape and more an embrace of the mundane.

The problem is that, on a basic level, a reader needs someone to care enough about, whether positively or negatively, to be invested enough to keep reading; he needs to know whose story it is, which characters to sympathize with, if for no other reason than to have a perspective he trusts. The heroes and villains of fairy tales and myths would be scorned by many today as facile and one-dimensional. But these tales have lasted thousands of years; the modern, meticulously realistic novel, on the other hand, is often out of print in two years. The ancients knew that such one-dimensional characters have great virtue. They can be a solid, unwavering element in a sea of changing waters, and actually enable you to let your other characters be more complex, more multidimensional. It is like the rope that trails a cave diver: As long as that rope is with him he can venture ever farther, take endless twists and turns; but without a rope to guide him, even the simplest turn can leave him hopelessly lost. George Lucas knew this when creating his characters in *Star Wars*, who come about as close as any modern characters to sticking to the ancient model of heroes and villains. They are black-and-white (literally). Even children can understand. And yet adults are enraptured, too. Children by the millions ran out and mimicked Darth Vader and Luke Skywalker, waving lightsabers and wearing the masks for Halloween.

The answer is not one-dimensionality. The point is, while crafting multidimensional characters, keep in mind the virtue of one-dimensionality and ask yourself what you sacrifice as you stray from that model. Real multidimensionality is a powerful tool for layering a character and bringing him to life. But it must be done sparingly, deliberately. In order for a character to withstand a blot, he must first be deserving of sympathy. It should be a stain on a sterling record; for a villain, it must be an accolade set against a treacherous history. Always ask yourself if you're reaching a point where the reader will be too confused about whether to be in sympathy with this character or not—or more, important to even care. If a character is endearing enough, we can both love him and hate him, be perpetually confused by him, and yet never want to stray from his presence.

EXERCISES

• **Scene List.** If you haven't already, make a scene list. List, chapter by chapter, the basic events or circumstances in the work. If you are still in the early stages it's okay if it's rough, even if it comprises only a few events or fragments of events.

• **Frequency of Appearance.** Now take your scene list (or, if you have a hard time with that, then make a simple table of contents) and beneath each scene (or chapter) write down the names of the characters that appear (or will appear). Now you have a list of specific character appearances in the work. Often revelations can come to light simply by virtue of this exercise. For instance, you might now realize that Character A appears in Chapters 1, 2, 3 and 5, but doesn't appear again until Chapter 14. You can instantly see if a character is evenly spread out throughout the work, or if his appearance is disproportionate. There is nothing necessarily wrong with disproportionate character time, as long as it is intentional. Often, though, it is not. A book or screenplay can be very long, and writers often lose perspective on who appears where.

This exercise also serves as an important first step in making an outline of the work, which we will discuss later.

• **Character Interaction Circle.** Take all of the characters in your work and put their names in one giant circle. (If you haven't written the work yet, this circle can be speculative—might even help spark ideas.) Draw lines that connect the characters who interact with each other—a straight line if they are friends (or on the same side), and a wavy line if antagonists. What revelations come to light? Do A and B only interact with C and D? Who else might be an interesting person for A or B to interact with? Who interacts the most? The least? What are the strong parts of the circle? The weak parts? There is no proper answer, no correct route, but it is essential that you have an overview, since getting a handle is not as obvious as it seems, and can especially be difficult in longer and more heavily populated works.

• **Setting Up Circumstance.** Knowing your character's makeup as you do, now is the time to draw on it. Make a list of ten things that might elicit a reaction from him. For instance, if he can't swim, place him on a small, rickety boat; if he hates loud people, force him to wait in a bar with five loud customers behind him; if he is a jealous type, have him show up at a party to find his wife dancing with someone else; if he is a dog lover, have someone give him a puppy for his birthday. Choose ten different circumstances—negative or positive—that will set this character up for a peak experience.

Now think of how each of these circumstances can be the core of a scene.

Now choose ten more circumstances that will set him up for a peak experience, but are also in line with the overall theme of the work.

Now think of how each of these circumstances can be the core of a scene that can move the work forward.

• **Character Action List.** Ultimately, we must judge our characters by their actions. The character who spends 400 pages thinking of how he hates everyone, but with his sole action helps an old lady cross the street, must be judged favorably. Conversely, the man who thinks of everyone with love for 400 pages, but with his sole action picks someone's pocket, must be judged negatively. Ironically, you'll find that by the sheer amount of time you've spent in his thoughts, you will probably still walk away with a judgment based on the thoughts, not the action.

Choose a character and do this exercise. Go through the work and make a concrete list of all of this character's positive and negative actions. Which side of the list weighs more heavily? Are you surprised to find a discrepancy between his thoughts, feelings, beliefs, and actions? How big is the discrepancy? How can we judge this person based on his actions alone? Is this what you'd expected? What changes can you employ to make this character more of who you want him to be?

• **Character Inspiration.** If you know the character you want to write about but are having a hard time coming up with a plot, stop for a moment and consider what inspired you to choose this character in the first place. What was it about him? What events or circumstances can help bring this out?

Chapter Four

The Journey

Writing a book is like driving a car at night. You only see as far as your headlights go, but you can make the whole trip that way.

—E. L. DOCTOROW

Hollywood studios test market their major motion pictures before releasing them to the public. They spend millions of dollars to gauge audience reaction, to find out, simply, if viewers are *satisfied*. What constitutes a satisfying experience? Is it universal? Is it something that can be manufactured? Why can't it suffice for us to watch merely a synopsis of a story? Why do we want to sit down with a five-hundred-page book or a two-hour film when we can get a quick summary of the facts, when we could know, up front, how it ends?

As you begin to tell your story, the first thing you'll find is that story telling is not about giving away information but about withholding it; the information itself is never as important as the path you take in disseminating it. It is on the traveling of this path that the reader or viewer will find his satisfaction, as for a bicyclist, it is in the biking—not the parking—that satisfaction comes. The destination, we find, is never as important as the journey itself.

The task of the writer is to create characters that can propel and sustain such a journey, it is to create characters on the verge of change, characters that will, in some way, be unrecognizable by the end of the work. *Ripe* characters. The man whose marriage is on the rocks and is ready for an affair; the mobster who has been careless and is ready for his downfall. The ideal character is like a volatile compound: unstable, unpredictable, a hair breadth away from either curing all disease or causing mass destruction. This is why Stanley Elkin says he "would not write about someone who is not at the end of his rope." We must remember that satisfaction and resolution would be impossible without first having dissatisfaction and lack of resolution.

Why is it some journeys satisfy us and others don't? A character might journey in a highly visible way, might travel twenty countries and age fifty years, and yet we might not feel moved; conversely, he might journey in the smallest, least noticeable of ways, and yet we can feel utter satisfaction. The answer lies in the nature of the journeys. Not all journeys are the same. There are the overt, easily relatabale journeys— what I call the "surface journeys"—but there are also, beneath the surface, the inner, less recognizable journeys— what I call the "profound journeys." As we begin to dissect them, we find that the difference between them can mean the difference between satisfaction and boredom.

Let us begin by looking at the three profound journeys:

Profound Journey # 1: Realization About Others

We listen to and interact with others all day long, but rarely do we *hear* them, take them for who they are; instead, we create an image of who we want them to be. We might unconsciously skip over their faults. We can wear blinders for many reasons: A mother might, our of pure love, refuse to see the evil in her son; an employee might, out of fear of security, refuse to see the fraud taking place in his company; a soldier might—indeed has to—refuse to see the good in his enemy. Sometimes faults are indeed seen, but are then justified, dismissed, diminished.

Seeing other people for who they are is not as easy as it may seem; to wake up one day and remove your blinders and acknowledge something for what it is (especially if it has been harmful) is, at the same time, to acknowledge that you had been wrong in your judgment. It would force us to face ourselves, to travel down the road of self-realization. This, for most people, is scarier than anything; many would rather live with the harmful person than come to such an admission about their own judgment.

So we live, instead, with blinders on about others. Until one day, if we're lucky, we can wake up and see people for who they really are. The abused wife finally wakes up and realizes what a jerk her husband is; the employee realizes what a jerk his boss is; the cult member realizes his group really *is* a cult; the rebellious son realizes his mother has always been good and kind to him.

While realization about others is a profound journey in its own right, it is still only a partial journey. The abused wife might get rid of her husband, but a year later fall back into the old relationship, or find an equally abusive husband; the cult member might finally leave, but might end up in a new cult a year later. Removing the symptom does not necessarily break the pattern. To do that, the person would need to embark on an even more profound journey: that of self-realization.

Profound Journey # 2: Self-realization

The character who embarks upon the journey of self-realization will not only realize that his group is a cult, but will go one step further and recognize that something inside him led him there; the battered wife will not only realize her husband is abusive, but will also realize she has always been attracted to abusive relationships. These characters will take personal responsibility for the relationships in their lives. Once they reach that point they might set new limits, not allow certain treatment anymore. Others will either have to conform to their wishes or leave. In one sense, they are coming to a realization of who they are and what they're really worth.

Why is remorse so important to us as a society? If someone has committed horrendous acts and is facing the death penalty, why should we even care if he feels remorse? What difference does it make? It makes a great difference for many people, because remorse signifies the journey of self-realization. This journey is held in such high regard that many people will be satisfied simply knowing that a criminal feels remorse—some will even pardon him based on that alone. Indeed, many religions hold that a criminal's entire fate in the afterlife—whether he can be redeemed, whether he ends up in heaven or hell—depends on whether he takes this inner journey. It is not accidental that the journey (or anti-journey) to remorse has been the crux of many works, from *The Stranger* to *Dead Man Walking*. Remorse itself is not significant—but the journey of self-realization is (Raskolnikov in *Crime and Punishment*).

It is possible that self-realization can be triggered from within. The ponderous thinker or recluse might come to self-realization through his own efforts. But often self-realization is triggered by an outside source, such as listening to a teacher, or being moved by a priest. Something clicks, and one realizes something deep within oneself. These outside sources are important catalysts, although one must remember that the fifty other people in the classroom or church heard those same words and didn't come to any self-realization. One must also be ready and willing to hear something, and this can only come from within.

Profound Journey # 3: Taking Action Based on Realization

It is one thing to finally realize what a jerk your husband is; it is another to file for divorce. It is one thing to realize that you have attracted a pattern of abusive relationships into your life; it is another to make a conscious effort to change your life's pattern, to seek therapy, to say No when the next one comes around—to *take action* based on that realization. The audience will get satisfaction from the realization alone, from, say, a killer's remorse. But they will get even greater satisfaction from the killer's being remorseful *and* dedicating his life to helping other victims. They will get satisfaction from the employee realizing his own company is crooked; but they will get greater satisfaction if, as a result, the employee decides to quit. A character can feel remorse, and think kind thoughts, and have a powerful self-realization, but at the end of the day, when it comes time to make a judgment on this person, we are left only with the trail of his actions, like dots on a map. Indeed, one could even argue that a realization is not a true realization if it is not followed by action.

In order to determine if your character might take action, you must first take into account the depth of the realization. Has your character changed beliefs after only listening to a one-hour speech? Or has he changed beliefs after having spent four years educating himself on an issue and carefully pondering it? You must also take into account your character's personality. Is he whimsical and easily impressionable? Or is he stubborn and hard to influence? A person who is constantly attending New Age seminars and comes home as a changed person once a week won't surprise (or satisfy) us if he comes home changed yet again; on the other hand, the man who has ranted against New Age philosophies his entire life but one day decides to attend a week-long retreat will satisfy us greatly. This man has journeyed.

Not going back to the old way of doing things is also a form of action. There is tremendous temptation for the former alcoholic to return to alcohol, the former gambler to return to gambling. Since we are creatures of habit, saying no to an old way of doing things is a powerful journey in and of itself.

Taking action based on realization is the most profound

of all journeys. At the end of such a journey, one is left with an entirely different character, unrecognizable from the character he had been—unrecognizable even to himself. (Now we see the importance of creating a character with the potential to change.) Beliefs come hand in hand with identity: All he need do is change his beliefs and take action based on his new beliefs, and he is an entirely different person. Whether he decides to join the army or dodge the draft depends entirely on his beliefs. When a son brings home a new girlfriend, what makes his parents worry is not the amount of time he'll spend with her but whether her beliefs will influence his, and thus change him into a different person—one who chooses not to spend any more time with them. This is why among the scariest of all works are those where the characters' beliefs are forcibly thrust upon them. It is no accident that what we remember most vividly about *The Manchurian Candidate* or *A Clockwork Orange* are the brainwashing scenes. These characters have become different people—involuntarily—and it is as if the original characters have been lost forever. It makes us realize how vulnerable we are to becoming different people.

Discrepancy between Realization and Action

Is it fair, though, to completely discount a character's realization if the character doesn't subsequently take action based on it? Can there be any mitigating factors? Shouldn't we also take into account whether the person has the disposition, willpower, confidence, or ability to take action on his realization?

Action is not always so easy, and we can't necessarily invalidate a realization without it. Often, other characters will try to sabotage a character's taking new action with comments like "this isn't you," or "this won't last," or "you've tried this before," or "you're going through a phase." This is because watching someone transform is scary; they might be left with a new person, and have no idea where they'll stand with him. They also might begin to worry that everyone else in their lives might change, too. Suddenly, life becomes much less secure.

A girl who is raised in a religious family and realizes one day that she doesn't believe in her religion might continue to stay where she is, still go through the rituals, or she might leave her environment completely. Given that the approval of her entire family and neighborhood is at stake, to leave would show great strength of conviction and character; but to stay would be understandable, even if she is living a lie. But does that make her realization any less of a realization?

It is possible for there to be a discrepancy between realization and action—in fact, there often is. Instead of hurrying to resolve this discrepancy—by having your character instantly take action—you might use it to your advantage and prolong it, thus creating one of the most profound forms of tension. The character knows what the proper action is but is unsure whether he can take it. He battles himself. The tension, if prolonged, can become unbearable.

This internal conflict can be the source of many psychological neuroses, like projection and paranoia. One can actually make oneself ill in such a case, can physically manifest symptoms. In extreme cases of religious guilt (where one sees oneself as perpetually in the wrong by not fulfilling the rituals and commandments) one can manifest such bizarre symptoms as bleeding palms or even demonic possession. It all goes back to the discrepancy between realizing the wrongfulness of one's actions and being able (or willing) to take the action to amend it. (In some cases, as with religious guilt, we must wonder whether such a realization of "wrongfulness" is a "realization" one would even want to have.) That is why hit men, Nazis, and other such types cannot allow themselves to see the wrongfulness of their actions. Once the realization kicks in, they would quickly be crushed under the burden of their actions.

The discrepancy can also be the source for a moral dilemma. What if someone comes to a realization of wrongfulness, but is *forced*, by reason of external circumstances, to continue his evil actions? Take the Jew who, at gunpoint, is forced to help the Nazis if he wants to spare his own family's death. Which comes first: murder or family? What if one realizes the crookedness of his company, but needs to keep working there to pay for his sister's operation? Where should the greater loyalty lie? To family or to strangers? When are wrong actions acceptable? How are they justified? What price will he pay for the sacrifice?

It is possible, too, that one can never resolve the discrepancy between realization and action. In fact, your work could be a study of the difficulty (if not impossibility) for most people to take action; one can realize his company is crooked and never take any action. You could leave it at that, leaving us with the partial satisfaction of his having had the realization. There are other ways you might make up for it and create satisfaction, even with his never taking action. We will, for instance, get a partial satisfaction by watching him torture himself under the burden of his wrongfulness. This self-burden can, as mentioned above, be used to segue into various psychological neuroses, even insanity—even suicide—and the work can become less about his taking action and more about the burden of inaction.

Inaction due to weighing consequences (as mentioned above) can offer a moral dilemma that can bring a sort of philosophical satisfaction, as readers can argue over which is the proper course to take and wonder what course they would take themselves. Most satisfying of all, you can have the character come to a realization and resolve to take action—even begin the action—but have it be too late. The employee resolves to turn in his crooked coworkers, but on his way to the FBI is arrested himself. After a particularly bad argument, the willful, contrary son finally realizes what a hard time he's been giving his mother and how good she's always been to him; he goes to her house to apologize, but finds her dead. (Flannery O'Connor's "Everything That Rises Must Converge") He has had the realization; he has resolved to take action; he has set out to take it—but it is too late. The action can never be taken. And yet, as readers, we still feel a sort of resolve, as if he *had* taken the action. This ploy is used for greatest effect in the genre of tragedy, going back to *Romeo and Juliet* and beyond.

The Surface Journey

A "surface" journey is a journey that is recognizable to all, a traditional, societally accepted marker of growth and progress, like losing fifty pounds, or climbing within one's company, or a new, blossoming romance. These journeys serve great purpose—they are journeys the reader can understand, relate to, point to if quizzed about the character. Is he an Associate editor? Editor? Senior editor? Does he make $35,000 a year? $45,000?

These journeys can easily be mistaken for profound journeys. They are not. These surface journeys are much easier—and more comfortable—to get a handle on than the profound journeys of realization, internal identity, belief, and resolution. The profound, internal journeys are, ironically, often viewed as less substantial, less permanent; whereas most surface journeys, like the gaining of a house, are considered more permanent, more stable. The tragedy of human life is that we allow ourselves to be distracted by these surface journeys and believe them to be the profound journeys. Possessions and ranks come and go, and ultimately it is the internal journey that remains (The Book of Job). If handled properly, though, the surface journey can be a pivotal tool in leading a character toward a profound journey.

Novels and screenplays are short mediums. We have only 300 pages or two hours to create a character, show him journey, change, and come out a new character. This is hard enough. How is one to achieve all that in such a short period of time and also not make it seem hurried? The surface journey can be instrumental in this regard: the romance that happens overnight, the man who wins the lottery . . . As we examine seven of the more common surface journeys below (in order of how quickly they can change a character's life), we'll see how rapidly they can effect a character change.

Surface Journey # 1: Romance

Given that it is the task of the writer to create quick—and believable—character arcs, romance can be one of the most powerful tools. Romance can change a character's life instantaneously—and, equally important, do so in a totally believable way. A character who just meets someone and starts dating will suddenly spend a lot less time with family and single friends. Indeed, it will impact his life in ways he cannot even conceive. How does the romance change family dynamics? Friend dynamics? Does he now spend most of his time at her place? At new places? Among new types? Of course, a journey needn't always be positive. A negative journey can have just as much—if not more—impact. Is he going through a separation? A divorce?

Most important, how can this surface journey lead to one of the profound journeys of inner realization? Often, couples become like each other. Might he become like her? What traits will he take on? Are his horizons broadening? They say that we would never allow someone to change us if there wasn't something inside us that wanted this change. Does he gain confidence with the new girlfriend and suddenly realize all of the things he is capable of? Does he act on these realizations? Reject all of the people who had been negative influences in his life? Or does he lose confidence with the new relationship? Is she constantly undermining him? Is he now meek and unsure of himself? Is he aware of her negative influence? Who is she like in his life? A mother, father? Is he repeating a pattern? Is there any chance of his breaking free? It is often, unfortunately, the negative surface journey that prods people to reflect and more likely leads to a profound journey. When the relationship ends, perhaps he is left with a big hole in his life, and can reflect on who he is without her; on how she made him change; on what is truly important to him. For some, a negative journey can become a positive one; for others, the resulting epiphany becomes too unbearable and the character is doomed to repeat the pattern.

Romance is also one of the more significant of the surface journeys in that it, potentially, leads to another important surface journey: family.

Surface Journey # 2: Material Gain

This surface journey is powerful in that it can also happen overnight and change a character instantaneously. Indeed, the journey of material gain has sustained entire works. Someone who comes into a huge inheritance, or wins the lottery, will watch his life change (at least on the surface) overnight. He can now buy the house, the car, travel the world—he no longer has to work! His day-to-day schedule will change. He will be free to spend his time as he chooses. The illusion is that the person's inner life will change, too; but sadly, this is rarely the case. Whether material success truly changes one's life will depend on whether he uses it as an opportunity for inner growth and realization.

How might the surface journey lead to a profound journey? Certainly, coming into a lot of money can make the character realize a lot about others around him, as they all clamor for a piece. It is more likely, though, that realization will come with material loss. The man who has his house burned down, or who loses a fortune in the stock market, or gambling, or in a lawsuit, will likely be more reflective. After a time, he might come to see what is truly important in his life. Will his priorities shift? Will he spend more time with his family, less time chasing money? Will he give more to charity? Or will his journey be negative? Will he become forever hardened and bitter?

Surface Journey # 3: Friendships

Friendships can change a person's life, and can do so quickly, especially in the case of people who meet and become friends right away. Indeed, some friendships can be stronger than family relationships. In middle school, high school and, to a lesser degree, college, friendships can feel all-important. In the business and political worlds, friendships (dubbed "contacts" or "relationships") can translate into millions of dollars. Friendships are a powerful surface journey, in that they can, believably, happen anytime, anywhere, and change a character's life from the start. Is the friend a positive influence? Does he encourage the character to broaden his horizons, read new books, listen to new music? Or does he have a negative influence? Does he rope him into fights, bring him out drinking every night, get him to curse with as much frequency as he does?

Enemies can also have a great impact on a character, and can also form quickly. If it is your character's first day in prison and he has slighted the wrong person by mistake, then he has suddenly made a powerful enemy who can haunt him throughout the entire work. Some works (*My Bodyguard*) are constructed entirely around the notion of fending off enemies. What does your character learn about himself by combating these enemies? What tactics does he use to fend them off? Does he even fend them off? Does he gain a new strength he never had before? What sort of enemies has he attracted? Does he attract them with frequency? Is it time to wonder if it is he? Or is he a victim of circumstance? (This is discussed at greater length below.)

Similarly, his joining a group—a gang, a company, the army—can change a character overnight. Does he now talk their lingo, take on their ethos? Watching him change can yield great satisfaction for us. How does he change? What does he learn about himself as he does? Does the army teach him inner strength? The company teach him that he's a born salesman? The gang teach him that he can fight? Is he excommunicated from the group? Why? How, if at all, does he differ from the other members? How can that lead to a profound journey? If the group falls away, what has he learned about himself? About others? How might he change his life as a result?

Surface Journey # 4 Physical

The changing of the body is a powerful surface journey since it can happen relatively quickly, is something everyone can relate to (and struggle with personally), and because it has the added benefit of changing the physical appearance, which many people, unfortunately, equate with identity. Indeed, the getting in shape or training of a character has alone been the crux of many works (*Rocky*). Does your character gain twenty pounds of muscle? Lose fifty pounds of fat? Become a champion swimmer? Shave his head? Get a tattoo? With such tactics, a character can quickly become (at least outwardly) unrecognizable. This alone can give a reader (and especially a viewer) satisfaction.

Illness, too, can provide a fast and believable arc. Your character can start out healthy, get diagnosed with cancer, and die within a short period of time. Or, he could be diagnosed from the beginning and fight the cancer and get better. He could be in an accident and lose his memory (*Regarding Henry*); he can lose a limb (*Born on the Fourth of July*). Physical changes have a special impact on the reader. In lesser works, this will suffice to carry the work; in better works, it is a means for one of the more profound journeys. What does he learn about himself? Does he learn that he can transcend bodily handicaps? Does he start to question who he is without his fully functioning body?

Surface Journey # 5: Knowledge

The gaining of knowledge is a noble endeavor and can provide, at least on the surface, the basis for a character's journey. In works like *Lean on Me*, the fight to gain knowledge sustains the work; in works like *The Chosen*, the Hasidic boy's gaining secular knowledge is dangerous and disapproved of, and is used as a catalyst for his doubts about his own community—ultimately, it is what makes him leave. A character might gain a formal education, he might learn a new language, or a special skill (plumbing, dancing, computing). The knowledge journey is unique in that it complements most of the other surface journeys—for instance, the man who works toward and gains the law degree also takes a journey of material gain since he will ultimately get a higher-paying job.

Unfortunately, though, knowledge or education is often confused with enlightenment, wisdom, or realization. One can fill one's head with every fact in the world and yet not necessarily come to any realizations about oneself or others. The Harvard professor, while extraordinarily knowledge-able, is not necessarily a sage, and not necessarily in touch with himself or others. Conversely, the Zen master with only an elementary school education might teach the character more about himself than anyone else he has ever met. Indeed, the ardent pursuit of external knowledge can often become a distraction from the much harder inner pursuit of realization.

Surface Journey # 6: Stature

Rising in a company often means an increase in salary (material gain), but it also means an elevation of position or stature. If an important executive rises and a newspaper runs the story, rarely will the newspaper extol the man for his rise in salary—it will mention his elevation in rank or stature. Material gain can come from nearly any source, but stature is a collective recognition that can come from fewer places, and is usually harder to come by. It is often an acknowledgment of power over other people, one of the highest forms of power there is.

This holds true whether one rises in a company, in the army, in politics, in a social association, or in a host of other fields. Generally, such a journey is prized, since it is long, slow, and not easily won. Indeed, if someone somehow reaches the top without such a journey, the reaction will often be skepticism and resentment. Think of the owner's son who is suddenly vice president after having worked for only one year. This journey is something people take great pride in; many will gladly labor on the low end of the ladder for years so they can boast how long and hard they worked to get where they are.

Can gain in stature lead to one of the profound journeys of realization? Doubtful. Rarely will a middle manager sit back and reflect on the days he was a stock clerk; rarely will the CEO want to reflect on his days as vice president. For most, stature often feels too tenuous to have the security to sit back and reflect on how things were; they had rather forget those days and see themselves as they are now.

Loss of position or stature, however, will likely lead to realization. The danger of being elevated is that people create an image of the elevated person; people inherently want role models, they want to imagine that the people they are answering to are greater than they are, if for no other reason than to justify why they are subordinating themselves. They can fantasize and project grandiose images onto the person and treat him as if he were greater than he is. If enough people do this long enough, the elevated person might start to believe it. When he comes crashing down, he will be in for a tough realization. He will be forced to realize his true identity is not one and the same with that temporary, elevated position. He might realize the danger of getting caught up in the glory of stature and get back in touch with who he really is. What changes will he make as a result? How will he start his life over again?

Surface Journey # 7: Family

A character who starts out with no children and has three by the end of the work will (at least on the surface) be a different person; so will the character who gains a brother (by birth or marriage), a sister, an uncle, a cousin. While family feels like the most permanent thing in the world, it is, in fact, always changing. There might be constant births, deaths, marriages, divorces. A character might have a huge family and spend all his time with them in the beginning, but not spend any time with them in the end. Perhaps he is excommunicated. Perhaps his wife has pulled him away.

Family is one of the crucial surface journeys in that it is most conducive to eliciting one of the profound journeys of realization. For the most part, family is not something one can easily escape, and one learns that if he is to live with certain family members, he must look inside and come to realizations about himself and others.

Still, family in and of itself is often mistaken for one of the profound journeys. Indeed, it can be a distraction from them—an easy, convenient distraction, since it is a giant, life-long undertaking and is often a noble, satisfying endeavor which will feel like a profound journey. It is not. This becomes most evident with "empty nesters," parents who've spent their entire lives raising their children and suddenly feel empty when their kids are all gone to college. They must realize, for the first time, that they have used their kids as a distraction from their own inner lives. The kids move out, their lives must go on, they are back to ground zero.

Family is not a profound journey. It is a surface journey. Realization is the profound journey. Empty nesters will now either find a new distraction, or they will look inside. For many, this time of life also coincides with retirement, another surface journey ended, another compulsory time to look inside—especially since there is little likelihood of starting a new family or a new job. For some, looking inside—the thing they have been avoiding their entire lives—is so unbearable that they choose instead to die. It is not coincidental that many illnesses and deaths coincide with these life-altering events.

Journey and Circumstance

Say your character returns home to find his house burned to the ground, or that he loses his entire family in an earthquake. His life has changed in an instant, but can this be called a journey? One might be tempted to label it a negative surface journey in the areas of material gain or family. But in actuality, in cases such as these it would be more apt to make a distinction between one's journeying and one's being the victim of circumstance.

If as a result of such traumatic events your character is plunged into despair, comes to deep realizations about himself and others—for instance, that he didn't need all those possessions anyway, or that he never got to tell his father he loved him—and changes his life as a result, then, yes, he has journeyed. But what if he does not? What if he walks away, dry-eyed, never gives it a second thought, and goes back to life as usual? Then, even though his life has changed, we must insist that he has not taken a journey.

How might external circumstances influence or spark a

journey? In the above example, a character's losing his house or family should certainly spark something. But it can also be less extreme. Perhaps your character never exhibited a religious impulse but one day visits Israel and is deeply affected, and as a result becomes religious. The same holds true with other people who cross your path. Perhaps Character A, a white supremacist, is forced to room with Character B, a black scholar. By virtue of this circumstance, perhaps A eventually befriends B, learns tolerance, even admiration, and leaves a changed person. In this case, the external circumstance has forced an internal journey that Character A would not have taken otherwise.

On a religious level, the Judeo-Christian schools of thought teach that God is just and that everything happens for a reason, even if we can't always see it at work. The Buddhist law of Karma insists that the universe is just, and says that to truly understand Karma at work, notions of right and wrong must be considered over the course of many lifetimes. Looked at in this light, what seems like a random, senseless act of injustice—like losing one's family in an earthquake—might be considered just: Perhaps in another lifetime this character had thrown someone else's family into a volcano. According to these schools of thought, then, on some level, there is no random victim of circumstance: Your character becomes responsible for all that happens in his life, whether he originates it, or it finds him.

Specific Goals: In all the above journeys, it is helpful if the character, before he sets out, has a specific goal or objective. In some cases the character will just stumble into a romance, or will have a new sibling born in his family, in which case he has journeyed without having a goal. But in other cases, a goal can be empowering and lend structure and direction. For instance, for a romantic journey, let's say he has a specific girl in mind; for a physical journey, let's say he knows he wants to reach 150 pounds; for a journey of knowledge, he wants to achieve a college degree; for a journey of stature, he knows he wants to be CEO; for a journey of material gain, he wants to have one million dollars in the bank, a particular house, a certain car.

Once one starts thinking of goals, one realizes there are many other, less tangible, journeys characters can take. There are journeys of principle. A journey for revenge. A journey for justice.

Destinations: Many writers know how their work will begin, but not as many know how it will end. A few writers write the last scene first, and some writers work in reverse, but for most writers the idea of such an approach is unnerving. Many writers have a great idea for an opening, or a great idea for a character, and want to let the work evolve. And isn't that what they're supposed to do? Isn't a work supposed to evolve out of a character? Wouldn't it be wrong to force a character to follow a preconceived path, to fit into a preconceived ending at any cost?

The answer is yes and no. It is true that a work should evolve out of a character, but at the same time one can also run into danger if his character wanders aimlessly with no destination, if his work doesn't build to anything and concludes with no resolve. So which path to take? As King Solomon said thousands of years ago, the answer is moderation. True, you should not force your character into an ending at any cost; but at the same time don't set him off running with no destination. His destination can be vague. It can change. Many writers fear having an ending will box them in. On the contrary: By virtue of having it, the character can become more creative within its confines. It is like putting your character on a train bound for California. If he decides to get off in Arizona, that's fine. If it turns out he should settle there and never get back on the train, that's fine, too. But he never could have known about Arizona if he hadn't first gotten on that train for California—if he hadn't had *some* destination in mind.

If you tell an actor to just get onstage and improvise, with no rules and no guidelines, he will likely be at a loss. But if you tell him he has only three minutes and by its end he must steal something, he can set to work without a pause and will likely be much more fluid and creative. Nearly always, the more rules, the more structure, the better the improvisation—the more confines he's given, the less he has to worry about everything else and the more he can focus on the moment. Indeed, what most people don't realize about improvisation is that it is extraordinarily structured. Actors are often given very strict rules about who they are, where they are, what they are doing, how to begin and how to end.

The same holds true for your character on the page. When you have a destination in mind, you can stop worrying where he'll end up and exert more energy on his getting there creatively. The journey will become richer. Knowing what to expect, you can even begin to play against the destination, perhaps with an unexpected route.

If having one final destination for the work is too intimidating, you can start by breaking the work up with several, smaller destinations. You might plan a series of mini-journeys. Where might your character be by Chapter 4? By Chapter 10? Also, you needn't necessarily think of destinations solely in terms of circumstance; you might also think of destinations in terms of internal character growth. What insights will he have reached by the book's end? In fact, it is always preferable to have an internal destination as opposed to an external one. An internal destination will create the external circumstances to get him there. An external destination will force him to a place he may or may not reach internally (often not).

Beginnings: Destinations are important. But so are beginnings. In fact, in one sense it is even more important to pay attention to beginnings since, when people think of journeys, they naturally think of destinations. Beginnings are nearly always overlooked, or taken for granted.

A strong beginning can define an entire journey. Think of someone who wants to get out of the ghetto; someone who wants to get out of debt. These people aren't thinking of destinations as much as they are getting away from their beginnings. Indeed, many driven, successful, accomplished people—people who have seemingly "made it"—are still fighting to get away from their lowly beginnings: Although the circumstances of their poor upbringing are no longer a reality in their external world, these circumstances are burned so deeply into their inner world it is as if they existed yesterday. They still fight an invisible fight.

A strong enough beginning will necessitate a character's journey away from it. Indeed, a character raised in the ghetto has one advantage over a character raised in middle-class suburbia: The ghetto character knows what he must get away from. His journey, even if single-minded, is laid out for him, and he needn't waste energy on worrying about other destinations. The suburban kid, on the other hand, is often relatively content with his surroundings and lacks the burning desire for a destination. Endless options lie before him, none propelled by necessity. This creates an angst the likes of which the ghetto kid could never know, an angst strong enough to be paralyzing. On top of this, the suburban kid might be derided for having everything and doing nothing—unlike the ghetto kid, who has nothing and might do everything. As Kierkegaard says, there are two types of despair: one of no possibility and the other of infinite possibility.

Some works can be entirely about their beginnings. In *Escape from Alcatraz*, we don't wonder if the inmates will end up in a mansion—we just wonder whether they'll get away from where they are. Where does your character begin? In a lousy job? In a bad neighborhood? On a desert island?

Obstacles: Obstacles are one of the most helpful tools at a writer's disposal—they help prolong any journey, help create unresolve, they cause conflict, and they aid in suspense. *Indiana Jones,* one of the highest-grossing films of all time, is prolonged entirely by obstacles. The protagonist has a mission, a goal, and we watch as new impediments consistently get in his way.

Even the simplest task can be infinitely complicated by obstacles. Say all your character needs to do is talk to his teacher on the other side of the classroom. He approaches, but his friend stops him and asks him a question. He answers and continues his approach, but then three other students surround the teacher with their own questions and he must wait. When it's finally his turn, the bell rings, and the teacher runs from the room. Your character chases him down the hall, but then before he can catch him, he slips on a wet floor and is knocked unconscious. . . . Through the use of obstacles, we have taken the simplest, dullest objective and made it exciting, even suspenseful.

For each of the types of journeys, you must consider what can stand in the way of your character achieving his journey. What obstacles lie in the path? What might impede the romance? His not having a car? A disapproving father? What obstacles might impede a rise in stature? A rival politician? An enemy who smears him in the paper? What obstacles can impede a journey to material gain? Do new, unexpected bills come in, just when our protagonist is about to break into the black? What lies in the way of his dropping down to 150 pounds? Does he suddenly get injured at 152 pounds and gain back ten pounds while holed up in bed? What lies in the way of his gaining knowledge? Can he not afford college?

Destiny: On a more profound level, we might also ask how fate or destiny plays into a character's journey. Destiny is not quite the same as destination. Take the King Arthur legend, where Arthur, as a boy, is told it is his destiny to be king. This impacts the entire work. We don't how or where or when he'll be king, or exactly what he'll be king of, and we don't know what his being king will eventually lead to—so there is not necessarily a clear destination—but there is a destiny. Destiny can add a sense of mystery and suspense, as we wonder exactly how and when he will be king, if *this* is the moment that will lead him there, if *this* is the person who will mentor him. It implants something in our minds which colors our entire reading of the text. It also adds a sense of direction, and most important, a sense of the inevitable.

This touches on a much more profound issue: There are schools of thought that state that in real life, everything is destined, meant to be, that your fate is mapped out before you are born. This is why a psychic can tell you your future, why an astrologer can make accurate predictions. It is a notion widely held; witness the millions of people who check their horoscopes daily. If this is the case, are we all just puppets on a string? Is there free will? Or are we operating under the illusion of free will? How does this affect your character and his journey?

You needn't have something as overt as the three witches in *Macbeth* prophesying your character's future from the offset; but you might imply a destiny. Say a character is born into a wealthy family, an only child; his father runs an empire, and all indications are that the son will one day run it. This, on a more mundane level, is his destiny. Destiny needn't always be on such a grand scale. Say another character is an only child in his forties, single, and lives with his mother, in her eighties, to whom he is very close. Let's say she is beginning to lose her capacities. Neither of them has money for private nursing. The mother is opposed to moving into a nursing home, as is the son. You might say it is this character's destiny to live with and watch over his mother until her death. His destiny, for the next ten or twenty years, is mapped out for him.

As you can see, destiny is powerful in that it can instill a strong sense of direction and purpose. The more layers of destiny, the more you'll feel your characters heading toward something. You might also play against this. Does he fight his destiny? Does the magnate's son spend thirty years rebelling against his father and the business world? You can bet that every moment the son rebels he thinks of his father's empire; he is acting *against* something. Even if he never gives in, you'll notice how it is always there in the background, how his life is defined as his *not* giving in to his destiny. Can he map out his own destiny? Build his own empire, bigger than his father's?

Interdependent Journeys: In *Rocky*, Rocky has many journeys, including the journey of getting in physical shape (becoming a better boxer), the journey of getting in mental shape (overcoming his self-doubts and taking seriously the possibility that he can be heavyweight champion of the world), and his budding romance. There is an interesting point in the movie when, depressed, he stops training. What is actually happening here is that his second journey (mental shape) is impacting his first journey (physical shape). We see that the two depend on each other.

Finally, it is his girlfriend who turns him around. The third journey (romance) impacts the first two. These journeys all run parallel to each other, and are well timed. If Rocky had reached the mental standstill earlier in the work, before he had met the girl, or when he didn't know her that well, then she couldn't have been there to propel the other journeys at the right time. The other journeys run their course as far as they can, and when they run out, she picks up from there. They are like sprinters handing batons to each other. The journey that ultimately propels us to the finish is the girlfriend; without that, there would be no more training and no heavyweight bout. Thus it is fitting that when the bout is over, Rocky ignores the reporters and calls for her; that the final shot of the film is of the two of them. *Rocky*, ultimately, is a romance.

In the above case, the journeys assisted each other. But can journeys conflict with each other? Can one journey be an obstacle to another? It is not uncommon for someone on the journey to becoming a rock star to also be on a journey into drug and alcohol addiction; for someone on the journey to stardom as an actor to let the fame go to his head and also begin journeying toward being an arrogant and self-centered person. Conflicting journeys can be powerful in that the conflict can help lead to one of the profound journeys of realization. The character ultimately must realize that a positive journey is taking him down the road of a negative one. He reaches a point where the two cannot coexist. He either gives up the drugs, humbles himself, or heads into self-destruction.

A powerful variation of interdependent journeys are parallel journeys. In *Shakespeare in Love,* there are two journeys occurring simultaneously, each feeding off the other and leading to the same place. In one journey, Shakespeare writes furiously to complete his play; in another, he courts the girl. The two converge when her love gives him the inspiration to write the play, and his writing gives her the inspiration to love him. One could not be without the other. They each combine to give us one greater, stronger sense of journey. In *Back to the Future,* the protagonist has separate journeys in the present and in the past, and each, as we find out in the end, affects the other; this is what lends this work its peculiar sense of satisfaction. In *The Matrix*, if the characters are killed outside the Matrix, they will be killed in the Matrix;

then again, if the characters don't achieve what they need to in the Matrix, they will be killed outside the Matrix. Each is rushing headlong for closure; each is dependent on the other.

The Journey That Leads to a Journey: One problem with resolving a journey is that the reader feels he has taken a ride, the ride is over, and he can now walk away. One way around this is to create journeys that offer resolution, yet also, by nature, spark new journeys, like a roller-coaster ride that seems to end with a false dip but then rises again, to even greater heights.

In actuality, most journeys spark new journeys. Let's say the character finally wins the heavyweight championship of the world. Then what? Now he has a whole new set of issues to face: defending the championship, staying in shape, combatting age, not letting fame and victory go to his head, becoming a spokesperson and role model, learning how to say no to requests, saving money for the future . . . These journeys may not be as exciting, but they are still journeys.

The goal is to create and resolve journeys that are satisfying but also leave you on the cusp of spawning a new, equally exciting, journey. This is why *Rocky I* and *Godfather I* and *Star Wars I* spawned successful sequels: They were completely satisfying, and yet at the same time left room for entirely new journeys. This is one of the most difficult things to accomplish in writing. It is looking ahead while keeping your eye on the road.

One way of doing this is to put the character on a journey we don't necessarily like. Let's say we watch as he becomes the best criminal there is. A part of us doesn't like this, since we know it's wrong and is bad for him, but a part of us—the part that needs a journey at any cost—wants to see him take it to the full extent, to see where it ends up. With Tony Montana in *Scarface*, we know his journey is dangerous, reckless, and will eventually destroy him; yet we want to see him take it, need to see where it leads. Take the journey of someone young and impressionable, being led astray by a cult. We watch him become indoctrinated, brainwashed, journey to become a cult leader. The journey is resolved, and yet we feel it is not resolved. We know it was the wrong journey for him and wait for it to come crashing down so we can watch him journey once again.

Previous Journeys: You should also consider if your character has taken any previous journeys before the work began. Take the character who used to be alcoholic and is now sober. This previous journey creates a sort of tension—the tension of *holding on to* the journey. There is the constant fear of his slipping back into alcoholism. What's old and familiar—like the old house or neighborhood—has a magical pull, and we soon see that his not going back to the way things were is a journey in and of itself. In this case, *stasis* is the journey. For most, stasis is too unbearable. Unfortunately, the Mafiosi who is released from jail and decides to turn his back on a life of crime will likely, eventually, slip back into what's familiar. For the Mafiosi, who is used to millions of dollars, the high life, action, and anything he wants, living a calm, quiet life is the most unbearable journey of all.

The Journeyless Character: Must every character in a work journey? What about a butler who makes three-second appearances? And if everyone is always journeying, won't we be left with constantly shifting sands? Don't we need some-one to remain the same, as a measuring stick?

Not every character need journey. Obviously, it takes time, energy, attention, and precious space to portray a char-acter's journey, and this space cannot be devoted equally to an infinite number of characters—if so, we would be at a loss as to whose story it is. Just as a reader can only follow so many characters, so, too, a reader can follow only so many journeys: If you overtax his attention, he might feel over-whelmed and follow no journeys at all. Additionally, the fewer journeys there are, the more significant they will seem. The journey, like all of writing, is about context. If your pro-tagonist is the only one coming to a realization in a world of unthinking zombies, he will get the attention. In one sense, then, some journeyless characters are necessary.

Looked at another way, though, everyone, however minor, should be journeying in some direction. A boy can journey, rebelling against his parents, and his parents can also journey—either becoming increasingly tough on the boy or coming to a realization that they have been wrong and asking the boy's forgiveness. In either case, the parents' jour-neys do not overshadow or detract from the boy's; if any-thing, they complement it.

As a rule, any character who is significant (remember that significance is not necessarily denoted by space) should be on some sort of journey—positive or negative, complementary to others' journeys, or as an obstacle to them, major or minor, subtle or overt. The journeyless should be reserved for insignificant characters, those who make minor appearances, or those dealt with *en masse*.

Other Types of Journeys: Next time you watch a film, pay attention to the cuts—specifically, to the length of the cuts. You'll notice that usually the opening, establishing cuts can be quite long—sometimes as long as ten or twenty seconds for a single shot. But when this same film reaches an action scene, you'll find the cuts changing as quickly as once a second. Unconsciously, the cuts work on us: They give the film an illusion of speed, tell us when to relax and when to tense up, when to settle in and when to get ready for change. By way of the cuts—and music and lighting and a host of other elements we don't pay conscious attention to—films journey on many levels.

The same holds true for the novel. An overt example is a work which uses generally longer sentences suddenly employing a series of short sentences. The content isn't changing; but our reading experience is, and this will, subliminally, affect the content itself.

The most skilled writers know this and use the text itself to complement the journey. If, for instance, a work is about a character's breakdown and is being narrated in the first person, you might find a breakdown of the character's ability to tell the story. Perhaps sentences will become fragmented or trail off or become impossibly long. Look at your sentence length, paragraph length, chapter length as the book progresses; look at the use of style, the use of language, the use of (or lack of) dialogue in key moments. Does the text journey with the story? Do the two complement each other?

Why the Journey?

All this talk begs the question, on the most profound level, why we, as readers and viewers, need a journey at all? Why do we crave—even demand—it, of our characters? Why is it that, without it, we walk away unsatisfied, angry? By attempting to understand, philosophically and psychologically, the human need, we might, as writers, be in a better position to satisfy it. There are thousands of possible answers; below, let's touch on four of the more obvious:

Inspiration

In some instances, we simply want to be inspired. If we are told that A is president of a company, that will likely have little impact on us as far as feeling we might reach that position, too; but if we watch A rise from an entry-level position, watch him climb through the ranks, overcome adversity—watch his journey—then we can visualize his path and perhaps feel that we might do it, too. It is the journey that allows us to connect the dots from the impossible to the possible, that can inspire us to take the same path. Nearly everyone wants some sort of change in his life, and wants an example to know it's possible. When we see a Rocky pull himself up from the streets, we get hope that we can do it, too.

Catharsis

The ancient philosophers raised the question: Why do we need art at all? Plato answered that we don't. He saw art as a bad thing, something that stirred up the emotions which, in turn, could cloud reason. Aristotle, on the other hand, saw art as necessary. Its chief function, he said, was to provide its viewer with a catharsis, to purge him of pity and fear, the two lowest emotions. The viewer could then return to normal life pitiless and fearless, ready to tackle anything. For Aristotle, the catharsis is the very reason for art.

Such a catharsis would be impossible without a journey. Readers need to go through the ups and downs, experience the traumas, revel in the successes; they need to live vicariously and finish a work having purged their own fantasies, ready to return to normal life.

Change

Life can quickly box us in with its routines, habits, obligations. Think of your day today; it was probably frighteningly similar to yesterday. The more settled we become in our jobs, homes, towns, families, friends, the harder it can become to envision a different life. More often than not, change can feel more like a fantasy—something that happened in the past or might one day happen again. This is why we get such a rush the first week on a new job, in a new house, with a new girlfriend, having a new car. We are reminded that change is possible. It is an affirmation of free will.

This is also why we love to see characters journey, change.

As we watch others change, we also see what is or is not acceptable for ourselves, what we hadn't considered. On the deepest level, the journey, which fulfills our need for change, can be seen as a giant distraction, a way of avoiding our own mortality.

Purpose

There are few things more satisfying in life than a sense of purpose. It can bring the worst enemies together in a common cause; it can propel people to work eighteen-hour days for years on end; it can cause a man to care for his mother for twenty years of his life and not give it a second thought. People want to rally behind a cause, want to be a part of building something. A country comes together in no greater way than in a time of calamity; if there is a flood or bombing, help pours in from all over the country; workers will stay on hand for months. Nationalism reaches its peak when a country is at war. Theories abound that, if one looks at history, one will find a major war breaking out every thirty years; if things lie stagnant for too long, a war must break out somewhere. In one sense, these thirty years can be seen as a buildup of purposelessness. Once it reaches its peak, the greater purposelessness is too unbearable for mankind—just as it is too unbearable for the individual—and wars are launched. Few things rival the purpose of fighting a war, or rebuilding from one.

Just as in life purpose gives the human being the greatest satisfaction, so, too, on the page, satisfaction comes with the purpose inherent in the journey.

<u>EXERCISES</u>

The Journey Outline

Take your scene list (building on the exercise at the end of Chapter Three), and beside each major event or circumstance, write down (or chart out) where each character stands in his inner journey of realization. Does he progress throughout? Does he do so evenly? Can his realization be stretched out? Condensed? Saved for one event? Stretched over three? Who changes the most? Who the least? Should certain events trigger more change? Certain events less?

Now look again at your list of events and circumstances, and this time ask: Could any of these events have been the product of inner character realization? Throughout the work, are events triggering realization, or is realization triggering events? Are there any events that can be added as a result of realization? How would that change the work?

Finally, look at each moment of realization and ask yourself, what, if anything, was the catalyst. Another person? A shocking event? Are these catalysts given due importance throughout the work? Is there no single catalyst? Was the realization cumulative?

Surface Journey List

How many surface journeys do you utilize in the work? Reflect on the seven categories described throughout the chapter: romance, material gain, physicality, friendships, knowledge, stature, family. Does he journey in all of these areas? Why or why not? If not, should you add them? If so, are there too many? Are there multiple journeys in each area? Do the journeys complement each other? Detract from each other? When does one stop and another begin? Do they overlap? At what point in the work? Why there? Which of these journeys leads to a profound journey? All of them? None of them? Why or why not?

Surface Journey Speed

Consider the speed with which each surface journey occurs. Is your work primarily about one journey—say, a character's rise to president of his company—and thus, does this journey happen slowly, stretched out over the course of the entire work? Or is his rise to presidency really just a precursor for a long, drawn-out fall, and thus is it covered in a single chapter? Does the romance happen overnight? Or does it take thirty years to bloom? How much space do you devote to each journey in the work? A romance can happen overnight, and yet still be described over 300 pages; conversely, a romance can happen over thirty years, but be described in a single page. Where do you need quick arcs? Where do you need slow arcs? Should his rise to wealth be slow? Or should it happen instantly? Should he lose his grandfather after a long, drawn-out fight with cancer? Or should he lose him suddenly in a car accident? How would either route impact the character?

Chapter Five

Suspense

Emotion is an essential ingredient of suspense.
— Alfred Hitchcock

One can have undeveloped characters and weak journeys and a hackneyed plot, but if suspense exists, an audience will often stay with the work. They might walk away resentful, might immediately forget the work, but for those few hours you've got them hooked. This is because suspense, more than any other element, affects the immediate, short-term experience of the work. It is thus an excellent complement to slow-moving elements that give a work substance.

If used improperly, though, suspense is just a means in and of itself. In these cases, the writer creates characters and circumstances merely to conform to suspenseful situations, instead of the suspense arising naturally from the characters

119

and circumstances themselves. Suspense becomes the destination, when it should, rather, be an adjunct to the journey. Even in such cases, though, the presence of suspense is still a feat and shows promise, since it indicates that the writer is writing more for the reader than for himself. Indeed, if you look at modern "literary" short stories and novels (such as come out of many MFA programs and appear in most literary journals), what becomes strikingly clear is that many of them lack suspense. With their emphasis on realism and metaphor, these writers seem to have forgotten that readers still need suspense, that they won't just read for reading's sake. Most of these novels (if published) are rewarded by selling only a few thousand copies, while a master of suspense (like Stephen King) will sell several million copies. Profound literary writing and characterization needn't be incompatible with suspense. Only the modern "literary" writer has taken such a contrary stance; one glance at Melville's *Moby Dick* or Conrad's *Heart of Darkness* shows how highly truly literary authors valued suspense.

What is it that compels us to keep turning the pages of *The Rise and Fall of the Third Reich*? That makes our hearts pound as the snow accumulates in *The Shining*? At first glance, suspense seems like a mysterious, magical element, but fortunately, to analyze suspense is to approach somewhat more definite ground. Ten different readers will have ten different opinions when it comes to defining a character's journey, but suspense is something universally recognized. Indeed, viewers who walk away disliking a film will often still admit to experiencing suspense.

Suspense, ultimately, is about anticipation. It is about what we do *not* have, what has *not* happened. It is about the *process* of watching events unfold: Once the victim is murdered, the woman wooed, the suspense disappears. But while the victim is stalked, the girl courted, suspense looms. Suspense, simply, is about creating and prolonging anticipation.

How one does that is much more complex. Suspense comprises dozens of elements, each building on and dependent on the next. Let us begin with the creation of anticipation (it can't be prolonged if it doesn't exist) and start with twelve of the more obvious ways to do this.

Creating Suspense

1. **The Objective.** The first step toward creating anticipation is having an objective (or destination) in mind for your character. A killer sitting in a room by himself is not nearly as suspenseful as a killer chasing a victim; a jogger idling aimlessly on the corner is not as suspenseful as a jogger racing to the finish of a marathon. The killer and the jogger need objectives. Once they have them, we suddenly want to know if they'll achieve them. Anticipation begins.

2. **Raising the Stakes.** The objective is an important first step, but someone taking out the garbage has an objective and this hardly makes for heart-pounding suspense. One way to build suspense is to raise the stakes. Let's say the garbageman only picks up once a week, that he is honking outside the door, that our character has missed him for three weeks in a row, that his tiny hallway is filled with foul-smelling garbage, and that his

landlady is going to evict him if he misses the garbage
man again. The garbage truck is revving; it is beginning
to take off. Now the stakes are raised, and our character's taking out the garbage has suddenly become suspenseful.

So one way to raise the stakes is to increase the
importance of the objective. This is not quite as easy as
it sounds, since importance, we must remember, is relative. Take, for example, a book deal. For A, who has
always dreamed of being in print and has been trying
his whole life, a book deal may mean everything, may
lend meaning to his entire life. But for B, who is a professional collaborator and has published fifty books and
enters into a new book deal twice a year, a new book
deal might seem routine. Likewise, if a billionaire
secures a one-million-dollar book deal it could mean
nothing to him; whereas if a starving artist working
minimum wage lands a five-thousand-dollar book deal,
it could mean everything. "Importance" is relative.

So consider the importance it has *for your character*.
In this way, a seemingly mundane objective will gain
great importance and thus suspense. How badly does he
want it? How long has he wanted it? Take the para-
plegic who has been trying to move his finger for ten
years. For the first time, he can move it an inch. Our
hearts pound with suspense over what would, for any
other character, be insignificant.

Stakes can also be raised by considering the importance a character's objective has for other people. Let's
take our courier delivering a package of blood for a
dying man. For the courier himself, the outcome of this

objective has no special importance; but for the man receiving the package, it is a matter of life and death. Thus, for the courier (if he is like most people), the delivery of the package will also take on great importance— we often go to greater lengths for others than we will for ourselves.

3. **Danger.** Danger is a powerful way to increase suspense. Let's say a character has an objective to swim across a river. Let's also say the stakes are high: If he doesn't make it, he won't be able to journey on with his peers. This scene is moderately suspenseful. Now let us change the scenario so that this river is also filled with hungry crocodiles and dangerous currents, that 90 percent of the people who try for it don't make it, and that an army is chasing him, so if he doesn't try, he'll be shot. We have increased suspense by adding danger.

Keep in mind, though, that even danger is relative. For instance, if two characters are thrown into the water and A can swim and B cannot, the scenario is only dangerous for B. *Superman* is an excellent example of the relativity of danger (and thus suspense). We don't fear for Superman when he is in what would otherwise be dangerous situations, like a building collapsing, since we know it can't hurt him; but when he approaches Kryptonite we fear for him greatly, even though we wouldn't fear for anyone else in that situation. The writer needed the Kryptonite because, without it, Superman could never be in danger, and thus the overall suspense would be much less. So, for danger to be effective, it must be dangerous for your character personally.

Suspense also comes when other characters are in danger—especially if your character is trying to get someone else out of danger. It doesn't necessarily come in our worrying for the other person, but in our character's being involved in an immediate objective with urgency, high stakes, something he (presumably) cares about, and something that might become dangerous for him. If your character stumbles upon a man on the street being beaten up and decides to intervene, there will be suspense; still, there is not quite as much suspense as there could be, since we don't know if the victim, being a stranger, deserved it, perhaps instigated it, or even perhaps would resent being helped. On the other hand, if your character sees that the person being beaten is his brother, the suspense will suddenly be much greater. Now he can't walk away. Now it affects him personally.

Remember, too, that are many types of danger. There is sexual danger (when a pretty woman walks into a dangerous neighborhood, we don't worry about her being beaten up—we worry about her being sexually assaulted); medical danger (an illness, or a contagious disease, as in *Outbreak*); emotional or psychological danger (when a child is abused); spiritual danger (if a character is being dragged into a world of murderers and is becoming one himself).

Suspense also comes if your character is a danger to others. In such cases there is nonstop tension, since wherever he goes, we wonder if he'll strike. It is the suspense of following a murderer, of sharing his viewpoint as he cruises down Main Street and eyes the children walking home from school. We know what he's capable of. Likewise, suspense comes with our character being dangerous to himself. He might be reckless—speeding drunk on a highway, playing chicken—or he might even be suicidal. Such a character is both the perpetrator and object of suspense.

Finally, we must remember that danger is all about perspective. It needn't actually exist in the real world for us to feel it—it need only exist in a character's head. Take the paranoiac who is sure that people are chasing him, and starts to run. Although the people aren't really there, we feel the suspense as he goes.

4. **The Ticking Clock.** Adding a time limit goes a long way in creating suspense. If a student taking a test has as much time as he wants, it won't be nearly as suspenseful as if he had sixty seconds. A ticking clock can be used in select scenes—like in the classroom—or it can also be used to frame the entire work. Some works—especially action thrillers—are propelled by this alone. Twenty-four hours to save the president (*Escape from New York*); forty-eight hours to find the criminals (*48 Hours*); thirty days to spend all the money (*Brewster's Millions*), etc.

A clock needn't literally be a ticking clock. Simply going through your work and asking yourself precisely how many days or weeks or months transpire can be tremendously helpful. Many writers are out of touch with their time line, and it has been my experience that if you ask most writers exactly how much time transpires in their work, they'll be at a loss to answer. This is especially the case if time isn't a major factor in the work.

Why does your work transpire over three months instead of three weeks? Why three weeks instead of three days? Believe it or not, most works can accomplish just as much over a shorter period of time. In the process, a sense of urgency will be added. There will be suspense where there was none.

Even if you decide not to add a time pressure, it is enormously helpful to know exactly how much time transpires and what sort of use you make of it. It will help you get a handle on how much time you are allocating to which events, and in most cases, help you to better allocate this time. You will also be able to incorporate atmospherically the passing of time. For instance, knowing a certain event took place specifically on a Friday, you might incorporate your character getting off work early that day; knowing a particular event occurred during the summer, you might incorporate your character's not hearing his phone ring because of the hum of the air conditioner. These small details will help ground the work and bring it to life.

Remember that a clock in and of itself won't add suspense—it all depends on how you *use* the clock. The ticking clock is useless if the character doesn't check it; but if he is reminded of it at every turn, it can play a major role. In *Manhunter*, we are given a time limit in the very first scene: The detective has three weeks until the next full moon to find the killer. From the very first minute of the film, the pressure is on. The writer didn't even let that suffice; many scenes also have an additional time pressure of their own, for instance when the team of detectives have only twenty-five minutes to solve a complicated riddle before a newspaper goes to press. Each time pressure propels us through each scene, while the greater time pressure propels us through the work and lends it direction.

Equally important is your space allocation. As a rule of thumb, when you want to give a crucial scene the greatest suspense, slow down your work to nearly the actual time of its transpiring. If, for instance, there are five seconds until a bomb explodes, a film might spend an actual five seconds on the countdown.

5. **Inability to Take Action.** One of the most powerful forms of suspense comes when a character has an important objective, but is unable to take action. A killer approaches a girl from across a parking lot. She fumbles with her keys, but can't get the car door to open. He's getting closer. Our hearts begin to pound. Or a girl spots her rapist in a crowd and tries to notify others, but her voice dies, and she is unable to scream. What creates the suspense in the final scene of *Rear Window* is the protagonist's broken leg; he hears his would-be killer approaching, but is helpless to go anywhere. If he were able to descend the fire escape, there would be no suspense at all.

This also applies if the character is unable to take action to help someone else, if he is forced to watch helplessly as danger approaches. A man sits in a boat while fifty yards away his best friend swims for safety, trailed by a shark. Or perhaps the character takes action but it is hopeless from the start, like in *Pet Sematary*, where the mother runs to save her child from an oncoming truck although we know she can't reach him in time. This very principle lies at the core of *The Dead Zone*, where the protagonist is able to see the future but is unable to get anyone to believe him.

A character can also be unable to take action mentally, psychologically, or spiritually. For instance, say he is breaking into a safe, but has suddenly forgotten the combination: He is at a mental standstill. Or say he is not that bright and is being bullied intellectually by a snob, and is unable to respond. Psychologically, a mother could be faced with a severely depressed son but be unable to help him, and thus be forced to watch him sink deeper into a depression and ultimately commit suicide. Spiritually, a priest might have to comfort a woman grieving over a dead son, unable to give her any peace. In all these cases, the suspense is agonizing, since we want our characters to take action, but they are all unable.

6. **The Unknown.** Let's say a character has to enter a basement. In Scenario 1 he is told in advance that when he reaches the third step a man will grab his leg. Our character descends with the lights on, sees the man approach and grab his leg on the third step. Everything happens as planned, and there is little suspense. In Scenario 2 our character is told only that there is something in the basement, something horrific. He is forced to descend into complete blackness. He has no idea what to expect. As he goes, he gropes his way. Suddenly, something grabs his leg. You can bet he will scream. (And so will the audience.) When all is said and done, these are

the exact same scenarios. Yet Scenario 2 is suspenseful, while Scenario 1 is not. Why?

There is nothing more terrifying than the unknown. We can bear nearly any form of torture as long as we know what it is we are getting into. But keep us in the dark, give us time to ponder the possibilities, and the suspense will be unbearable. This is because our imaginations usually conjure up worse scenarios than will ever happen. Stress experts say that this is what stress is about—the anticipation of awful scenarios. They point out that when we actually experience an awful scenario—say a car crash—our stress level drops to zero. The scenario never actually causes the stress. It is the unknown that causes it.

The horror genre makes best use of the unknown— indeed, this is the crux of many alien movies. Is the alien friendly or dangerous? Are there more of them? It is not surprising that, of the top ten highest-grossing films ever made, many of them involved an alien being.

The unknown lies at the heart of works with supernatural elements. *Amityville Horror. The Exorcist. Poltergeist.* The supernatural works because it will always be unknown, because we will never quite understand what we are dealing with, even when human beings harness the power. *Firestarter. The Dead Zone. Carrie.* In all of these works the person with the power won't himself know very much about it, thus magnifying its mysterious nature.

The unknown needn't always be employed on such a dramatic scale; it can help cause suspense even in our daily lives. Take a character's first day at a new school. As he walks the halls, sees unrecognizable faces, we feel for him. What is he getting into? The suspense at that moment—when all is still unknown—is as great as it will ever be. Once he knows the school—the classmates, the teachers, the buildings—the suspense disappears.

The unknown can also make settings suspenseful. It is not the haunted house or the cemetery itself that is scary—it is not knowing what could be inside.

7. **Sexual Tension.** A famous filmmaker once said, "All you need to make a movie is a girl and a gun." Try to picture *Romancing the Stone* without the love interest. It would somehow be less complete, less dimensional. The action keeps us on the edge of our seats during most of the work, but the writer also knows that for the action to have the greatest impact, there needs to be a break. Instead of using these breaks for dead time, he uses them to heighten the suspense—just in a different way. Instead of navigating through a deadly jungle, Michael Douglas must deal with a more formidable contender: a love interest.

Sexual tension can create one of the most powerful forms of suspense. It can carry an entire work, and make up for little else happening. But simply having the romance there is not enough. Indeed, many writers make this mistake and assume that since the romance is in place and blossoms, they have done their job; this is why we end up with many hackneyed and staid romances. These writers forget why the romance needed to be there to begin with: to create suspense.

So how does one use romance to create suspense? There are endless possibilities. The forbidden romance is one of the most effective: The courtship of a married woman will create more tension than the courtship of a single one; two lovers who come together despite the disapproval of their families (*Romeo and Juliet*); incest is often too delicate for most writers to handle, but it can create the most powerful form of suspense. Romantic scenarios between a character in a position of authority and a subordinate can always create tension—a teacher and a student (*Private Lessons*), a boss and his assistant. So can a dangerous sexual partner (*Basic Instinct*).

What is most important to remember is that the suspense disappears when the courtship is consummated, when the lovers are content. To keep suspense, then, the writer must prolong courtship as long as possible, or have the lovers break away so he can have them court again. If all is well in their world, he must find ways to sabotage it. One powerful way is to create obstacles to their love: Perhaps they have gaps in age (*Lolita*), or geography, or race, or wealth, or education, or stature (*Pretty Woman*); perhaps the woman is already "reserved" for another man (*Shakespeare in Love*). In many ancient myths, the hero had to go through numerous trials—usually impossible and deadly—to win the woman he wanted. What does your character have to do?

8. **Dramatic Irony.** "Dramatic irony" is when we, as readers or viewers, are privy to something the characters themselves are not—often something that is about to affect them. A young couple swims laughingly in the

ocean, flirting and splashing each other. In the distance, a huge shark approaches. The couple, unaware, continues to laugh. Meanwhile, the shark gets closer. This is dramatic irony. It is not suspenseful for the characters. It is not suspenseful for the shark. It is a special form of suspense—designed just for us. And it works.

Dramatic irony is powerful because it actively involves the audience, makes them want to scream out in warning. It also makes them feel as if they were getting the complete story, getting to see angles the characters cannot. Dramatic irony could entail our knowing information that all of the characters do not (as in the above example), or it could also entail our knowing information that only one character does not. For instance, let's take our scenario of the courier delivering a package of blood for a dying man, and change it so that the courier doesn't know what's in the package, thinks it's paperwork. As a result, he strolls down the street, taking his time, browsing in the windows. Meanwhile, we know that the waiting recipient has only hours left to live.

Let's take another scenario, where our protagonist sits down for dinner with his girlfriend. There is no inherent suspense. Now let's change it so that we know his girlfriend is pregnant but he does not, and we know that she is going to tell him over dinner. Now there is suspense, and we sit waiting for the moment. Let's change it again so that we also know he is going to break up with her over this dinner, but she has no idea. Now every word, every gesture will be filled with suspense. A good writer will draw this out for as long as he can; he will fill the dinner with false starts, with hints, with interruptions, distractions, silences. He will torture us for the sake of suspense. He can afford to. It is a strong setup—because of dramatic irony—and he will milk it for all he can.

Dramatic irony can also be used to lodge us in a character's viewpoint. In the first scenario, when we only knew what she wanted to tell him, we sympathized with her, since we knew she was waiting for her chance. We felt for her every time she tried and couldn't, or was cut off. In the second scenario, knowing what each had to tell the other, we alternated our sympathy, although in this case we will probably feel more for the boyfriend, since he is the one that has to break the bad news (assuming she views the pregnancy as good news). If we were to change the scenario yet again so that we knew the restaurant was planning to poison them, our sympathy would shift to them as a couple, instead of as individuals. Viewpoint and dramatic irony come hand in hand.

Dramatic irony can also be used to create suspense in comedy—indeed is the backbone of most comedies of errors. Dramatic irony alone propelled the hit TV show *Three's Company*, where the landlord believed the main character was gay, while we knew he wasn't (but had to pretend to be in order to keep his apartment with the two girls). This made for hilarious situations, as we watched while the landlord preached to him about "manly" topics.

9. **Living in the Future.** We rarely live in the present. Instead, we spend much of our time worrying about

what we'll do an hour from now, tonight, tomorrow, next week, next summer—in other words, living in the future. We anticipate. Since creating suspense is about creating anticipation, why not draw on anticipation itself?

A simple way to increase suspense is to increase the sheer amount of time a character spends anticipating something. If a character goes onstage to give the biggest performance of his life, but doesn't give it a second's thought beforehand, we won't be nervous for him. However, if a character spends one hundred pages fretting about the impression he'll make on his girlfriend's parents, our hearts will pound when he finally walks up the walkway to their house—for no other reason than the amount of time he spent anticipating it.

Many writers spend little, if any, time showing their characters preoccupied by the future. In actuality, this could be a major part of any character's makeup—indeed, propel an entire work. In *Unfaithfully Yours*, the majority of the work is devoted to Dudley Moore's daydreaming about how he'll commit a murder, planning every last exquisite detail. In his dream, it all works out perfectly. By the end, when it finally comes time for him to execute his plans, our hearts pound with suspense. In this case, anticipation ends up being used for comedic effect, as every last detail goes horribly wrong.

This is also why we enjoy heist movies—we get much enjoyment in watching robbers make elaborate plans and then waiting to see if they will work out. Oddly enough, if everything goes perfectly, there is less suspense; in a sense, we want things to go wrong. This is because it gives the audience joy to watch the *difference between anticipation and reality*. In real life, we spend much of our time anticipating things that will never happen, making plans that won't work out exactly as planned. It is comforting to see we are not alone. As the old saying goes: "Man makes plans and God laughs."

Also keep in mind that page time is not real-life time. A character might have anticipated something for three years, but if his anticipation is only dealt with in one page, we will not feel it; conversely, he might anticipate for only a few hours, but if 100 pages are devoted to this, we will feel it greatly.

10. Lack of Resolution. Most works comprise many subplots. It is inevitable the audience will like some more than others, and when you force them to switch to a different one, you risk losing them, since you are, in effect, asking them to start all over again. One way to overcome this is to employ a lack of resolution—that is, to end a subplot at a crucial moment, leaving the audience dangling. The audience will then be in suspense while they are taken through the other subplots, always waiting to get back to it. This is a favorite gimmick of soap operas.

Lack of resolution can also be employed at the end of a work, to propel us into sequels; part of the reason *Hannibal* was such a commercial success was because *Silence of the Lambs* ended with the killer back on the loose; for this same reason *Halloween* was able to spawn seven sequels (and counting) and *Friday the 13th* even more. Of course, when it comes to the greater work you walk a fine line: If you end with a lack of resolution, the audience might also feel a lack of satisfaction, see through the gimmick, and resent you for it—perhaps enough to not pick up the next one. The challenge is to offer resolution to the greater story, to give the audience 95 percent satisfaction, but to also leave something without resolution, to leave some element that will cause 5 percent dissatisfaction—just enough to propel them to the next one.

Lack of resolution can also be employed in individual scenes. Say a man comes home excited, eager to tell his wife a great piece of news about work. They sit down, he is about to tell her, and the doorbell rings. It turns out to be his long-lost sister; completely distracted, they bring her in and a long dinner scene ensues. What helps propel this dinner scene is the lack of resolution from the scene that preceded it (his news) and our need to get resolution. Indeed, it can lack resolution in many ways—perhaps his wife, also, had a great piece of news to tell him. Perhaps they also had sixteen messages on their machine and hadn't had a chance to check, and they knew one of them would have more good news. . . . With so many loose ends, the audience becomes more invested in getting through that dinner—unless, of course, there are too many loose ends and not enough resolve, in which case they might just, in frustration, set the work down.

11. The Secret. If properly used, the secret can create enough suspense to propel an entire work. Whodunits thrive on secrets. Who is the killer? What isn't the butler telling us? So do soap operas. Who is she sleeping with? What is she holding back from him? In *Casablanca*, the secret Ilsa holds back from Rick is used to stretch the suspense from beginning to end; In *Psycho*, the truth about Norman Bates's mother is kept secret until the penultimate scene. If we had known the truth in the beginning, the film wouldn't have been half as memorable—or suspenseful. In *Casablanca*, if Ilsa had told Rick her secret up front, there would have been nowhere left for the characters to go.

For the secret to be used for suspenseful effect, we have to know there *is* a secret; Norman Bates's mother is alluded to in shadowy fragments; in *Casablanca* Ilsa flat out reveals there is something she cannot tell Rick; in the whodunits, we know from the long looks the staff exchange with each other that someone is not saying something. The realization of the secret brings no suspense; the suspense comes in knowing it is there while not knowing the answer. The greater its importance, the greater the suspense. The closer you bring the audience to knowing the answer, the more they'll want to know.

You must be careful, though, because the secret is a rather obvious ploy, and if overused or not used subtly enough, it can seem gimmicky and contrived. The secret is also unfortunately often used as a way to compensate for little suspense in other areas. The secret should complement other layers of suspense; it should not have to bear the sole burden of creating suspense.

12. **The Character.** The type of character you create can go a long way in helping or hindering suspense in the work. Horror films, for instance, need the character foolish enough to walk into a just-burglarized house and search the premises himself. We know (as anyone

would) that the burglar waits just around the corner, and we groan at his stupidity. But we also squirm as he creeps down the hallway. There would be no suspense if this character had, when he noticed the front door ajar, made a sensible decision and run for the police.

Your character might be heroic. Put him in front of a burning house and there will be suspense, since we know he is going to run inside to search for survivors. Or say your character is claustrophobic and has a complete breakdown anywhere near small spaces; arrange for him to have an important business meeting on the 53rd floor of an office building, where he will be forced into a tiny elevator. Or say your character is a fighter and is protective of his sister. Let him know his sister was just beaten up and our hearts will pound, since we know, by his character, what he will do (Sonny in *Godfather I*). Simple character traits can help add suspense to common scenarios, and the scenarios in turn can draw on the character's traits.

Similarly, not knowing a character can create suspense. You might deliberately suggest some element of unpredictability, some sense of mystery about him. This way, getting to know him becomes prized by the audience, and, more important, it creates suspense, since we never know how he's going to react. It is like watching two dogs meet on the street: They might love each other—or they might attack.

Say our character is a calm, likable person, but also has a temper and doesn't do well around bossy, authoritative types. His boss calls him into his office, starts criticizing him, then starts ordering him around. Given our character's makeup, the suspense starts to build. Will he explode? One of the elements that keeps *The Shining* suspenseful is that we know that, in the past, Jack Nicholson abused his wife and son. As the snow mounts, and the pressure builds, we know he's capable of doing it again.

Suspense also comes into play during a character's journey (covered at length in Chapter Four). The discrepancy between a character's coming to an inner realization and his taking action based on that realization can keep us on the edge of our seats. She decides she's going to throw him out when he comes home. He comes home. Our heartbeats quicken. Will she do it? Let's say she can't bring herself to; she decides, though, that she will the next day. This can keep us going for a while.

Similarly, suspense comes in knowing a character's destiny. Will he achieve it? When? How? At every turn we must wonder, is this the moment?

There are, of course, many other possible routes to suspense. The twelve above simply cover some of the major categories. Except for one: conflict. But conflict is so significant that it has a chapter in its own right (see Chapter Six), and so it will be passed over here.

Prolonging Suspense

Good writers know how to create suspense; better writers know how to prolong it. Creating effective suspense is not that easy, and the best writers know they shouldn't let it go once it exists. Many writers do the hard work of creating strong characters, settings, or situations, but then don't follow through with the easy work of developing them; and the writers who do achieve suspense often don't prolong it for half as long as they could. Part of being a good writer is being able to identify when you have a good thing—even if you've stumbled upon it by accident—and being able to adapt even if it means changing your original plans. For instance, you may have envisioned a work with a very quick opening scene, say of a murderer killing his first victim, as a sort of prologue to the greater work; however, when writing this scene perhaps you find that it is extraordinarily suspenseful. Most writers conform to their original plan; better writers, though, recognize what they have, change their plan, and go with it, even if the new material ends up comprising the entire first section of the story.

In the final scene of *Rear Window,* as our protagonist sits in a wheelchair, helpless to do anything but wait, Hitchcock chooses to have the killer approach excruciatingly slowly, his boots echoing off the stairwell. A lesser director would have had the killer run up the stairs and burst through the door. But Hitchcock knows he's on to something. There are many powerful suspenseful elements converging: danger, the unknown, the ticking clock (the police are on their way), the inability of the character to take action, and very high stakes (life or death). Prolonging the anticipation, he stretches the killer's approach to over thirty seconds of film time. He then prolongs it again: Once the killer opens the door, he does not enter, but stands there, encased in shadow. No one moves. Neither talk. The suspense becomes unbearable. Anticipation has been prolonged within the scene—indeed, we have been anticipating the killer since the start of the work.

Nearly all suspenseful elements can be prolonged. You can prolong danger in endless ways, even when you think you can't: A character can survive a dangerous operation only to develop a dangerous infection, or a character can get through one dangerous obstacle only to be faced with another (the crux of the *Indiana Jones* films). You might prolong the unknown by letting your character in on only some of what he's dealing with, solving only one of the mysteries of a haunted house. You can prolong sexual tension by having your characters a hairbreadth away from kissing, only to be interrupted—or have them break up after they consummate their relationship, in which case there will be suspense regarding their getting back together. And if anticipation is prolonged enough—with any of these elements—it can evolve into something much stronger: expectation.

Expectation is an extraordinarily powerful tool—in fact, it lies at the core of schools of thought ranging from a modern self-help course (Anthony Robbins) to ancient wisdom (Buddhism). Anthony Robbins says if you want something in life, it is not enough simply to want it: You have to feel entitled to it and you have to envision having it—you have to *expect* it. Buddhism, on the other hand, claims that many of our worries in life come from the fact that we expect things and are thus inevitably disappointed; for Buddhists, the solution is to let go of expectation. What is important is not who is right but the fact that expectation is powerful enough to provoke two entirely different schools of thought. Let's see how we might use it for our purposes.

Let's say your character daydreams of asking a girl out. Let's say he has been envisioning this for *years*, and knows down to every detail exactly how the scenario will go, with his approaching her and her joyously saying yes! After all this time, he will have this scenario so firmly entrenched in his mind that if one day he finally asks her and she actually says no, he will be shocked—might even feel betrayed, as if she's changed her mind. But she hasn't changed her mind—she had never made it up to begin with! His anticipation has evolved into expectation. What is important is that expectation has set our character up for a significant moment either way.

Prolonging is an art form in and of itself. Should every suspenseful scene in your work be prolonged to keep the reader on the edge of his seat for twenty minutes? Probably not. Like everything else in writing, it is about context. By prolonging the suspense in a particular scene, you intimate that that scene is more significant. When you prolong suspense, the audience will take it very seriously, will expect it to lead to something significant; if you force us to watch your protagonist tiptoeing through an empty house, only to culminate the scene in a cat jumping out at him, the audience will resent you for it and be less willing to become immersed in the suspense in the future. However, if the scene had only taken ten seconds, they will more easily forgive you.

Let's say a character took an important final exam and the results won't be posted until next Monday. Now the suspense can continue for an entire weekend as he frets about his future. Let's say he arrives Monday and it turns out the results will be delayed for three more days because the teacher's sick—the anticipation builds. Let's then say the results are posted on Thursday, but his aren't there; the teacher mistakenly left his at home. By that point, we are ready to kill the teacher! All by simply prolonging anticipation.

EXERCISES

• **Raise the Stakes.** Make a list of the characters in your work and for each character, ask yourself: What's at stake for this person? Have you created people who inherently have much at stake? Desperate characters? At the end of their rope? All of us have some desperation inside, no matter how content we may seem on the surface. What is your character's source of desperation? How can you bring it out?

Look at the major events in your work. What traits can you give your character that will help add suspense to these scenes? Or, conversely, look at your character's traits. What major events can you write that will play on these traits for maximum effect? What is his chief objective? What will happen if he does *not* achieve this objective? What will he gain if he does? Will it change his day? Or will it change his life? How might you raise the stakes?

• **Suspense Rating.** How much of a priority have you given suspense in your work? Is it in every scene? Is it saved for the end? The beginning? Go through your list of chapters, and on a scale of 1 to 10, rate each chapter's suspense factor. Are some chapters more suspenseful than others? Why or why not? How you can make less suspenseful chapters more suspenseful? How can you make the suspenseful chapters even more suspenseful? If suspense is not pervasive, what makes you think you can do without it? Are you making other aspects of your work (characters, dialogue, action) overcompensate? If your work is low on suspense, find the few areas where it is suspenseful. How can you expand on these?

• **Prolonging Suspense.** Go through your list of suspenseful scenes, and ask yourself how you can prolong each of these. As an exercise, take a suspenseful scene and make it twice the length, stretching out the suspenseful moment. If it is one page, make it two. Two pages, make it four. You can go back and cut it when it's done. What have you added by doing this?

• **The Unresolved.** Take each suspenseful scene in your work and find a way to turn it into two full-fledged scenes. Find a way to end the first scene so that it is unresolved, compelling the reader to come back to it at some later point in the work. (You have now doubled the number of suspenseful scenes in your work.) Can you apply this technique to any actual chapters? To the end of the work?

Chapter Six

Conflict

Any conflict, whether it takes place within the body or outside, is always a battle against the self.

—Taisen Deshimaru

As much as we may wish to ignore it, conflict is rife in our daily lives. Who has not gone through a day without a basic time conflict? Conflict is inherent in the very creation of the earth: The Earth is poised against the Heaven, the Waters are poised against the Land. The animal kingdom is all about conflict: Animals eat each other, fight for the same food source.

In one sense, life can be viewed as a series of choices: whom we choose to marry, how many children we choose to have, where we choose to live, where we choose to work, how we choose to spend our time. . . . Our choices dictate our lives. And every choice implies a conflict: If there weren't two (or more) conflicting options, then no "choice" would be necessary. For every choice you will make today there will be a conflict: what you wear (you could have worn something else), what you eat (you could have eaten something else), what channel you choose (you could have watched something else). . . . Some people will go to great lengths to avoid conflict. As a writer it is your job to embrace it.

Conflict serves many functions: It involves the reader by requiring him to take sides (and thus sympathize), it creates a rift that paves the way for resolution and satisfaction, it aids in suspense, it can lend a work a sense of direction, and it can be unexpected and thus create unpredictability. Conflict can also teach us about our characters: Who initiated the conflict? Who fosters it? Who tries to mediate? In *Othello,* we learn as much about Iago—the character who thrives off of the conflict—as we do about the subject of conflict himself.

There are endless forms of conflict—both inner and outer—and endless to ways to help create it. Let's look at thirteen of the more basic:

1. **The Characters.** If you choose the proper characters and situations, conflict will create itself. Your task is to create and bring together characters who are diametric opposites so that there can be nothing *but* conflict when they meet. When a general and a draft dodger are put in a room together, the conflict potential is high; likewise if you bring together a Holocaust survivor and a former Nazi. In *The Odd Couple,* a sensitive neat freak is forced to room with an insensitive slob; with such a powerful setup, the challenge isn't creating conflict—it is keeping it at bay!

If your characters are authentic (not types), then the

results might be unexpected. Let's say a gay liberal and a homophobic conservative are forced to room together; one would expect conflict, and indeed the potential would be high, which is good. But you also retain the choice to play against that. In real life, sometimes people who seem to be polar opposites are best friends. Perhaps these two characters find common ground; perhaps the gay liberal sets up his roommate with his beautiful female friends; perhaps the homophobic conservative is able to help his roommate with admittance to a country club; perhaps they both come from domineering fathers; perhaps they both have the same taste in music, movies, fashion, food. . . . Maybe, despite their seeming differences, they get along fabulously. (Also see Chapter Three: Applied Characterization.)

Regardless, the potential must exist. *Every character in your work must have the potential to conflict with every other character, whether that potential is realized or not.* This holds true even if they are best friends, even if they are lovers—even if they never find out about the other's source of conflict, and even if they never actually have the conflict. This way, you at least have the option; you also, more importantly, create another level of suspense for the audience, since they wait for the conflict to erupt at any time. Even if the conflict never erupts, it is far more interesting to watch two conflicting people get along.

Go through your list of character traits (the questions you answered in Chapters One and Two), and consider again your character's race, politics, money, status, education, profession. . . . Drawing on who he his, consider how you can create circumstances and other characters who can be a potential source of conflict for him. If he's a diehard Republican, is he snowed in with a Democrat? If he works for the IRS, must he spend an afternoon with a tax evader? If he plays football for Army, is he stuck in a bar filled with rival Navy players? In all of these cases, if there is to be conflict, it must be over something the characters care deeply about. For instance, if the Army and Navy players don't strongly identify with their teams, there will be no conflict. If the Army player alone cares, there can be trouble; if both care, most likely there will be trouble.

Characters with no innate reason for conflict might, of course, come to conflict as a result of the circumstance. Two gladiators who must fight to the death; two boxers who must fight for the title. But then you're relying on circumstance to create the conflict, and might end up forcing extreme circumstances in order to make up for weak characterization. Both are necessary, but, ideally, the circumstance will arise from the characters and not vice versa. If you find yourself working hard to create a conflict that isn't naturally there, then you know something's wrong. In such a case, it's time to go back and reexamine your character choices. (See Chapters One and Two.)

2. **Groups.** Groups of people—especially if united in a common cause or ideology—inherently demand conflict. Mothers Against Guns will conflict with the National Rifle Association; the Coca-Cola Corporation will conflict with Pepsi; the Bloods with the Crips.

What is even more interesting is how group conflict

trickles down to the individual. If you are to be a loyal member, you will have to make the group's conflict your own, personal conflict. If you are a Blood, you can't be friends with a Crip; if you work at Pepsi, you can't walk the halls drinking a Coke; if you are the chair of the Democratic Committee, you can't vote Republican; if you are a devout Jew, you can't take part in Catholic rituals. Of course, you *can* do all these things, but to do so would be betraying your group. Thus, a group dynamic *forces* conflict, whether it is conflict with the external entity, or conflict within. Most will choose conflict with the outside—even if they like Coke, even if they'd rather vote Republican—since at least in this case they will be guaranteed their own group's continued support.

One must also take into account how long this character has been a member of the group, how big a role it plays in his life, how loyal he is to it, and how strongly he feels about his group's stance on a particular issue. This is where it can get really interesting. If a character has just joined a group and it insists on his cutting off all communication with his family, chances are he will walk away from the group—the group's roots are not deep enough, and his family is too powerful a conflicting factor. But if this same person has been a dedicated member of a group (i.e. skinheads) for ten years, and all of his family members and friends are also part of this group, and all his time is spent with them, and the group gives him his sole sense of identity in life, and then the group demands he stop visiting a peripheral acquaintance who is a Jew, he will likely conform to the group's wishes.

But what if he is faced with equal conflict between

the external and the internal, as often happens in real life? Take a cop. Let's say he has been a cop for twenty years, and all of his friends are cops, and he spends most of his time with them, and identifies with them—but suddenly finds out they're crooked, and strongly disapproves of their actions. What does he do? It is not so easy to turn one's back on a group, especially if entrenched. The collective approval, identity, and way of life of a group can make it harder to go against than a family.

3. **Forced to Be Together.** One of the most effective ways to heighten and prolong conflict is to take two (or more) conflicting characters and force them to spend time together. Perhaps they are forced to become roommates, cell mates, coworkers. Are they assigned the same barracks in the army? The same dorm room? Are they teammates? Stuck together on a desert island? Chained together? Two characters who want to get away from each other but can't can be powerful enough to propel an entire work (*Driving Miss Daisy*). What obstacles lie in the path of their getting away?

Of course, you must also take into account how deep the source of conflict is. Does A whistle and B hate whistling? In this case, their chances of overcoming their conflict are fairly high. Or is one a lifelong KKK member and the other a Black Panther? In such a case, their overcoming their differences is highly unlikely, unless one of them is willing to change.

It also depends on how much time they spend together and how close their quarters are. If the KKK member and the Black Panther are stuck together in a 12 × 12 cell for a year, they would probably eventually budge, even if in the smallest way. Perhaps they will never stop hating each other, but will at least work together to notify each other if a guard is coming. In the end, each must learn some tolerance and compromise; each will learn about himself and others; and each, if he can get past his petty annoyances (or superficial preferences), might come to see there is much more to the other than he had thought. Such setups can also be used to segue into a character journey. (See Chapter Four: The Journey.)

4. **Conflicting Objectives.** There is a traditional exercise employed by beginning actors of the Stanislavsky method. Two actors are placed onstage. The first is given an objective (i.e. tuning a guitar), while the second is given his own objective (i.e. hanging a painting), which requires the assistance of the first actor. The first, busy with his own objective, cannot comply. Inevitably, there is conflict.

We all want things in life, all the time. If we stopped and counted, we might easily have one hundred objectives a day, whether it's getting a seat on the subway or getting the Danish in the window. These are all possibilities for conflict. What if there's only one seat on the subway? Only one Danish in the window? What if another person is going for it at the same time? Suddenly, on a beautiful, sunny morning, there is conflict.

How characters deal with such conflict shows us a great deal about them. Does A concede the subway seat, happy to let B have it? Does B in turn decline the seat to A—or does B happily take it? Does A lunge for the open seat? Does B do the same? Do they argue over it? Actu-

ally come to blows? What is important here is that none
of this would be possible if there weren't an objective.

If the object of a conflict is a person (for instance, a
girlfriend), how the object reacts can also say much
about that person. Does she thrive off their conflict?
Does she foster it? Tell A all the bad things B said about
him? Sing B's praises in front of A? Or will she avoid
conflict at any cost? Does she choose one over the
other? Or choose neither, to avoid conflict?

5. **Raising the Stakes of Objectives.** Having conflicting objectives is an important start, but it is not always
enough. Often, to bring out maximum conflict, you
must raise the stakes of these objectives. Let's go back to
our two characters wanting the same subway seat. If
they are both just taking a casual, two-minute ride, that
seat won't be overly important to either of them, and the
conflict potential will be low. Let's raise the stakes. Let's
say A has been standing on the train for three hours
waiting for a seat. Let's say B, who has just boarded,
beats him to it. A might be indignant. What will he do?
Will he quietly smolder? Confront B? Use force?

To increase the importance of an objective, increase
how badly your character wants it. Increase how badly
the conflicting character wants it. Also increase its
rarity—if it is a one-of-a-kind van Gogh and two people
are bidding on it, the conflict will be much greater.

6. **The Power Struggle.** In one sense, the struggle for
power is the struggle for an objective. Power, like any
objective, is sought after and highly prized. When two
people want it, conflict occurs.

But power is unique among objectives: Unlike a subway seat, the person who gains it will dictate the lives of others, and whoever doesn't have it will have his life dictated by the other, which makes the stakes inherently high for both parties. Unlike a subway seat, power is always up for grabs—the person having it could lose it, and the person without it might get it. Additionally, power in and of itself is valueless; its inherent value comes from controlling others. Indeed, it is entirely relative: Without others, there is no power. Without subordinates, a boss is a boss of no one.

The power struggle is rife in everyday existence and can be tapped in endless ways. Its most obvious form is in a battle with authority—parents, police, the law, the army, the government (*First Blood*). In fact, it is rare to encounter the person who is one hundred percent joyous and content; most people feel oppressed in some way. Find the oppressed, and you will find the oppressor.

Once you've located the struggle, heighten the stakes; prolong it. Make the slavemaster harsher; the slave more oppressed. The conflict will reach a boiling point, a point where it *must* be resolved. The slave will have no choice *but* to take action—he will either rise up and kill his master, or he will be broken, will become meek and obey, his spirit crushed. Conflict doesn't come in oppressing or being oppressed—it comes in the *struggle* to break free.

Some individuals are defiant in the face of any form of power; but for most, conforming to some form of power is a part of daily life—indeed, a necessity. If we are to drive the streets safely, we all must yield to the power of the law in the form a red light; not every man can be CEO in a five-hundred-person company. Conforming in and of itself shouldn't cause resentment, shouldn't cause a struggle. What causes the struggle is the feeling by those who are subject to the power that they should have the power (for instance, a worker under an inept boss), or, more commonly, the misuse of power by those in power (e.g., a boss who yells at his workers or keeps them late though he leaves early). In such circumstances it is your job to tap into the power struggle and prolong the conflict for as long as you can.

7. **Competition.** A is approached by a small client, in whom he is hardly interested. But then A learns that his rival, B, is courting the same client. Suddenly, A is interested. Why? It is not about the client—it is about the *winning* of the client. What excites him is the competition. When two characters want the same object, it becomes about more than just the object. This is why a person might come to blows over something as petty as a seat on a subway: not because he's lost the opportunity to sit on twelve inches of plastic—but because he's lost the *competition*.

Competition is one of the few forms of conflict that is endorsed—even encouraged—by society. Capitalism thrives on competition; competitive sports are watched and encouraged by millions; even state-sanctioned schools are competitive. Companies know that if they make two (or more) employees compete with each other, they can produce greater results from each. This is because competition, while a source of conflict, can also drive people to greater heights.

Competition is also among the most primal of

instincts: Children will cry hysterically if their siblings or peers are given something (say, a candy bar) that they are not. We teach our young children to suppress their competitive instincts, that they should be happy for their siblings when they receive presents on their birthdays. Yet, paradoxically, when they get older, we encourage them to take part in competitive sports. We want competition—yet we only want it on certain terms, in certain arenas. We want to control it, to tame it, to make it predictable. Children thus repress their instincts—but they never disappear. As adults, all those years of repression can rear their head in ugly ways.

It is thus not surprising that competition often infantilizes people, and can bring out the worst. Some people react in strange ways when placed in a competitive situation. What drastic or unusual steps will A take to win? Is he competitive by nature? How might he react differently than usual when put into a competitive situation? Will A push an old lady out of his way in order to get the seat first? Will he yank B out of the seat by force? Does A become indignant if he doesn't get the seat? Will he throw a tantrum? Blame other people? Will he quickly forget about it, or will he stand there and glare at B for the rest of the ride? Does he get thrilled if he does win the seat? Does he gloat over it? Rub it in B's face? Competition can be valuable in teaching us about our characters.

When tapping competition, you needn't look further than everyday life: It rears its head in everything from team sports (football, baseball), to individual sports (boxing, tennis), to games (chess, cards), to the workplace (competing for a job, competing for a client), to relationships (courting the same girl), to family (competing for a parent's love).

8. **Time.** In one sense, life can be viewed as the use and allocation of time. For the busiest people, with the most demands on their time—parents of young children, CEOs of large companies, celebrities—time conflicts are a part of everyday life. For many, time is literally money, as many workers get paid by the hour. If a worker wants to spend a day at home, he will lose money and will thus have a time conflict. If a parent wants to go to his child's school play, but also has an important work meeting, he has a time conflict. Often, we are at the whims of other people's schedules when shaping our own.

A simple way to create a time conflict is to schedule two important events for your character at the same time. Your character will be conflicted as he debates his decision, and this, instead of being resolved, can be prolonged. When he finally makes his decision, there is more potential for conflict, as he, even while at the event, can wonder how the other event is going. Finally, when he returns from the event, there is even more potential for conflict, as he must deal with the anger of people associated with the event he didn't attend, and possibly he will feel remorse, and even regret, if he made the wrong decision.

Time of day can also create a conflict. A morning person and a night person travel together; each day the morning person is frustrated as the night person doesn't wake until 3 P.M. and each night the night person is frustrated as the morning person goes to bed by 11 P.M. Or a husband works the night shift while his wife works a day shift; they barely see each other, and their relationship begins to break down. A simple glance at our characters' calendars can often yield endless conflicts of time.

9. **Family.** Friendships come and go. Marriages break apart. But your primary family (mother, father, brother, sister) is permanent, whether you like it or not. Indeed, this is one of the defining factors of a family. Thus, on one level, family conflict is the conflict of people who are forced to be together (#3)—but taken to the extreme. For our purposes, you can exacerbate this by literally forcing them to be together—have them live in small quarters, have two sisters share a bedroom, a bathroom, or force two feuding brothers to attend endless family functions together.

The family can be a breeding ground for special forms of conflict not found elsewhere. Siblings vying for their parents' love and attention; siblings in competition with one another; a father in a power struggle with his son; children privy to their parents' fighting. There can also be conflict in accepting new in-laws: If two sisters are close their entire lives and then sister A gets married and suddenly no longer spends time with sister B, you can bet that there will be conflict between sister B and her new brother-in-law. A divorce creates tremendous conflict, including the conflict of accepting new stepparents or stepsiblings, and the ultimate conflict of forcing a child to choose which parent to live with.

What is perhaps most significant about family conflict—especially in the case of parent-child dynamics—is that it creates a pattern for conflict, especially when a character is involved in a conflict from a very young age, and particularly when this dynamic is the only model he has. The son who is used to battling with his father will likely battle with authority his entire life. In a sense, then, the family conflict is the conflict that lives forever.

10. Romance. Romance brings to the table its own set of conflicts. Lust and physical attraction can often blind a couple to each other's faults, to potential sources of conflict; eventually, though, the honeymoon wears off, and any suppressed conflict can come to the surface—sometimes powerfully enough to damage or even destroy a romance. There is inherent conflict if they each come from different backgrounds. A poor girl marrying a rich man won't necessarily be cause for conflict, but if the poor girl was raised with animosity toward the rich—and still identifies with her upbringing—then her animosity toward the rich is bound to one day find a victim in her partner. If he, in turn, was raised with disdain for the poor, there is bound to be even greater conflict. If he is Jewish and she is Catholic, there is not necessarily cause for conflict; but if they take their religion seriously and are practicing, then conflict is inevitable. Even if they reach a happy medium, the conflict will likely resurface when it comes time to raise their children.

Indeed, the raising of the children can be a great source of conflict—if he is strict and she is lenient, if she wants private school and he wants public, if he lets them watch TV while she wants them to read . . . Taking a step back, there can be much conflict over their deciding even to have a baby, when to have it, and how many to have. There can be conflict over choosing a

name. If it's an unwanted pregnancy, there can be conflict over whether even to keep the baby.

The blending of two families can also be a source of
conflict. Parents are often nervous about seeing their
children being married off, siblings are often worried
they won't spend time together anymore—on top of
this, each family is forced to meet a group of complete
strangers. The potential for conflict is high, especially in
the beginning, and particularly if they come from dia-
metrically opposite backgrounds.

Similarly, once they are married or dating, there can
be conflict over how much time they get to spend with
their own families, especially if they both come from big
families and if they each had been accustomed to spending most of their time with their own families before
they met. If additionally one spouse—or both—do not
get along with the other's family members, then the
conflict can be even greater. This also holds true for the
spouse's friends—if one dislikes the other's friends, it
can be cause for conflict, especially if the other spends a
great deal of time with those friends.

Time conflict can also be applied to couples. There
can be conflict if one demands a great deal of the other's
time, especially if the other is very busy or is used to
having more time of his own. There can be conflict in
how much time each spends away from the other (at
work, with friends). And there can be conflict in how
they choose to spend their time together—which movie
to see, which restaurant to attend, where to vacation.

For some couples, competition can enter the mix and
be a source of conflict. If the two met as struggling

actors and one of them becomes hugely successful while the other still struggles, resentment can build. Likewise if one starts earning more than the other; if one gains weight while the other doesn't. . . .

There can also be conflict between the couple and the outside world, especially if it is a union that is disapproved of—if he is forty and she is sixteen; if they are gay and living in a straight neighborhood.

Moving to the darker side, jealousy can be a source of conflict. If a man always perceives his wife as flirting with others—whether true or not—conflict will abound (*Othello*). If she fosters this—or does actively flirt— the conflict can be great. If a man abuses his wife— physically, verbally—the conflict will be severe; if she abuses him back, the conflict can become so tense that it might seem less like a marriage and more like a fighting ring. (Of course, this all depends on how it's handled— in *Three's Company,* for instance, Mr. and Mrs. Roper constantly make fun of each other, yet, because it's all done lightheartedly and because they offset the fighting by expressing their love for each other, their conflict becomes a source of comedy.) If a man is having an affair, there is tremendous potential for conflict—both between the man and his wife, and between the wife and the mistress (*Fatal Attraction*). Finally, there is the ultimate romantic conflict: divorce.

11. **Work.** The workplace can be a breeding ground for special forms of conflict. There can be conflict between workers for promotion or advancement; this conflict can be heightened if, say, only one person out of twenty gets promoted a year. There can be conflict between workers

for the same client, or the same business, or for taking credit for accomplishments; this can be heightened if the company fosters such conflict. The most common form of workplace conflict comes between a worker and his boss; this can be heightened if the boss is unfair. Conversely, there can be conflict between a boss and his assistant if the assistant continually makes mistakes. There can also be conflict between a worker and her company, if, say, she is at odds with their philosophy or way of operating. (*Norma Rae*)

There can be conflict between companies, both vying for the same client. There can be conflict between a worker and his own client, particularly if the client is demanding. An agent represents Actor A who generates $10 million a year and receives an offer to represent Actor B who generates $10 million a year. However, Actor A and Actor B are rivals, and Actor A threatens to leave if his agent represents Actor B. This agent has a serious conflict.

Of course, all of the other forms of conflict can be applied to the workplace as well. Time pressures (conflicting deadlines); romance (conflict between attracted coworkers, or sexual harassment); the power struggle; conflicting objectives; people who are forced to be together for an extended period of time; and family. Many business are family-owned or family-run, and this can breed more heightened conflict, as family conflict exacerbates work conflict.

12. Perspective. Let's go back to our two men in line at the bank. Man 2, if you recall, thinks the tellers are deliberately taking their time, to upset him. As he stands there stewing, waiting for his turn, the conflict builds. In actuality, though, where is the conflict? Have the tellers really done or said anything to him? No. The conflict *feels* real to us—as it must for this character—but in actuality, no conflict exists in the real world. It only comes from his perspective.

So many fights and miscommunications are based simply on people misunderstanding each other, on having different perspectives. Perspective can be an amazing tool to help create conflict out of nothing. If A says, "You look beautiful," to B, B might perceive A as being sarcastic and insult him back. A, who had been sincere, would feel he is being unjustifiably attacked by B and might insult her back. A fight has been created out of goodwill and skewed perspective.

13. Inner Conflict. As we saw with perspective, there needn't always be an external character or circumstance to create conflict. In fact, the greatest form of conflict is often inner conflict. External conflict, at least, is delineated and can be resolved, avoided or ignored; inner conflict, on the other hand, isn't so easily labeled, can never be avoided, and sometimes is never resolved. Indeed, it could be argued that we often crave—and even create—external conflict in order to take our minds off our inner conflict; the more innerly conflicted a person is, the greater the external conflict he will create in order to ease his inner burden. This is why some people can only truly relax when in the midst of a crisis—and will often go to great lengths to create one.

We are faced with endless petty inner conflicts every

day. Two brands of beer sit on the shelf; they both look delicious and are equally priced. Which do you choose? Some people might choose instantly, just to ease their mind of the conflict—such people might be labeled "impulsive." Others might debate for minutes, anxious to make the best decision—these might be called "procrastinators." What drives the impulse buyers and the procrastinators is the same thing: inner conflict. In this example it was harmless; but inner conflict can manifest with more severe ramifications. What if, for instance, the impulse buyer buys a three-thousand-dollar computer without comparing prices, just to get it over with; or if the procrastinator spends thirty minutes in the store staring at those bottles of beer?

Inner conflict can also involve broader, more substantial life issues. Take the woman who lives in South Dakota and is very close to her family, yet who also yearns to live by the ocean, to move to Florida. Her family would never move. She is deeply conflicted. No matter what she chooses—to live by the ocean, or to stay with her family—a part of her will never fully enjoy it, and she will always long for the alternative.

A character can also be conflicted ethically over whether he has acted properly. He could feel conflicted over religion, over whether he is following the rituals properly, or whether he should be following them at all. He might feel conflicted over his choice of friends, his choice in romance, his work, his living situation—any number of issues. All a character need do is feel innerly conflicted, and he can create the external circumstances

that bring him toppling down from CEO, from the perfect marriage, from fortune. Taken to its extreme, inner
conflict—especially that which cannot be resolved—can
literally drive people mad.

Prolonging Conflict

Creating a good setup, making the right choices, is half the
battle. The other half is the execution, the prolonging of the
conflict. Conflict can't be resolved too quickly, or else suspense will disappear; then again, it can't be maintained forever, or else the reader will feel a lack of resolve. The solution
lies somewhere in the middle. If you're dealing with a TV
series like *The Odd Couple*, you will need to maintain the
conflict for one hundred shows or more. Simply having a neat
freak and a slob won't be enough. You will perpetually need
to find new sources of conflict, new issues they can disagree
on, new quirks that annoy them. You will need to create new
situations and predicaments for them to induce fresh conflict.
The characters might bring old conflicts to new situations (a
father and son in a perpetual power struggle join a baseball
team and begin to argue over who bats first), or they might
first discover that they have conflicts based on these situations (two brothers meet a pretty girl they both like, and for
the first time realize they both like the same type).

But if we have only conflict, this can be overwhelming.
Like suspense, conflict is about contrast. We need some
resolve, some breaks to allow us to breathe and to prepare us
for the next bout of conflict. *The Odd Couple* would often

begin with an incident that created conflict, spend the rest of the show prolonging and heightening it, but end with its being resolved. This way, we had satisfaction. However, at the very end, there was often some other tiny—comedic—incident to create a new conflict, to show us their conflicting relationship was still alive, ready to explode, and to propel us into the next episode.

Equally effective is prolonging the *anticipation* of conflict, creating a situation where conflict is waiting to happen. You might, for instance, let the reader know that A is a former Nazi and B is a Holocaust survivor, although the characters themselves don't know it. They sit in a room and make small talk—perhaps even become friends. All the while, we wait for the conflict to erupt. Perhaps they never find out, and it never does. Perhaps it only comes out years later, after they are already best friends. What do they do then? This is the most agitating type of conflict—yet also the most profound—since it demonstrates that there is more to us as human beings than the temporary roles we have played or the identities we took on at certain times in our lives.

EXERCISES

• **Character Conflict Gauge.** How big a conflict-seeker is your character? Is he antagonistic? Argumentative? Does he always take the opposite side? Must he always stir things up? Does his profession reflect this? Is he a lawyer? A boxer? Or will he avoid conflict at any cost? Is he meek, passive? Will he always give in? Is he a mediator? On a scale of 1 to 10, how would you rate his potential for conflict? Having a good handle on who your character is will help you get a better handle on those he comes into contact with.

• **Collective Character Conflict Gauge.** Look at your cast of characters. How much potential is there for conflict between them? Have you made good choices collectively? Can you change them individually to create greater collective conflict? If the characters are happy together, what could drive them apart? Conflicting agendas? Different classes, races? Incompatible astrological signs?

Drawing on the Character Interaction Circle exercise (at the end of Chapter Three), consider which characters in your work spend time with each other. Do the characters with the most potential for conflict spend time with each other? Should your characters interact with different characters?

• **Objectives.** Take an ordinary scene between neutral characters and introduce a conflicting objective. Make the objective one of a kind. Create a desperate need for each character. Watch how the scene comes alive. How can you apply this principle to other scenes in your work?

• **Choices.** As we mentioned earlier, choice, by its nature, implies conflict. Look at all of the major choices in your character's life: marriage, kids, profession, geography . . . What was the conflict for each of these? Who else might he have married? Where else might he have lived? What other career path might he have taken? Our interest is not so much in what his life would have been like, but in drawing out the conflict of these pivotal choices. Does he spend his entire life

conflicted over two professions? Does he spend years commuting between his wife's house and his mother's (300 miles
away)? Can you incorporate any of these major life decisions
into your work? Can you prolong the conflict leading up to a
major life decision?

Chapter Seven

Context

Just get it down on paper, and then we'll see what to do with it.
—MAXWELL PERKINS

Sometimes I find myself reflecting on great scenes, terrific characters, amazing passages of writing. Momentarily puzzled, I try to remember what works they belong to. Then, in a flash, I realize, they don't belong to any published works. In my mind I carry a sort of graveyard of writing that never made it into print. In my role as editor, I've sometimes had to cut some of the best writing I'd seen anywhere, because it detracted from the rest of the work. This is the most painful type of editing, but great writers know that context is all.

There comes a time in writing when you must step back from the beauty of the individual word or line and make a judgment on its context within its sentence or paragraph. So, too, must you eventually step back from the individual scene, circumstance, character, or setting, and make a judgment on its context within the work. Writing is like a symphony: Nothing stands on its own, and everything must eventually be judged inasmuch as it aids (or detracts from) everything else.

While traditional editing requires your homing in on a particular line or paragraph, editing for context demands the opposite: Now you must zoom outward. Now is the time for a bird's-eye view. Especially if your work is long, editing for context will require great mental energy, distance, and objectivity, the ability to keep the entire work in your head at once. You must consider the overall impression on the reader. Not an easy task. It is, in fact, tricky, elusive, and changes with every change you make.

Context influences suspense, conflict, pacing, progression, and ultimately meaning. Too much suspense will drown out suspense, too much action will drown out action. Below, we will consider the context of each element of plot development by itself; then we shall consider the work as a whole. To begin with, let's consider the main issue when editing for context: repetition.

Repetition

When considering context, the most common edit is for repetition. Sometimes I'll edit a writer's manuscript and send it back with a scene cut and the writer, having only looked at the pages with the edits, will call and say, why did you cut that scene? It's a perfectly good scene. And I'll answer, yes, it is, but reread the entire work and you'll see this scene repeats the same theme (or characters or circumstances) handled in an earlier (or later) scene. On its own it's fine; in the context of the work, it needs to go. Invariably he'll grumble and guardedly agree to reread the work—and then come back two weeks later and agree.

Verbatim repetition of words and phrases and sentences is relatively easy to spot. Paraphrased repetition is less easy to spot, particularly if spread far apart; vague repetition of themes or circumstances or intention can be much harder to spot. The key to doing this is to read your work in one sitting, looking only for repetition. You must remember that you wrote your work over a long period of time; it is highly likely that, with all the stopping and starting, you repeated yourself at some point, even in the vaguest way.

Also keep an eye out for repetition of characters. Are there two or more characters in the work who are too similar? If so, they can detract from one another. Can they be combined into one? Or, does one character appear too often? Also look for repetition of settings—do we keep coming back to one setting? Are all the settings so similar they are hardly distinguishable? In such a case, how might you add contrast? Also look for repetition of action or similar events; repetition of similar character journeys; and repetition of scenes. Always ask: Does this scene really add to the work? Is it *that* different from the ones that preceded it?

Sometimes the audience *needs* repetition. There is a lot of information for a reader to absorb in any given work—names, facts, dates, places, settings—and it is quite likely the audience will forget some things as they progress. Thus, if there is a significant fact in your work—especially if it is glossed over and especially if it is a long work—you might want to, subtly, remind the audience at some point. This type of ploy is often found in detective works, where some small detail glossed over in the beginning comes flooding back to the detective in the end. The audience will remember and will be glad for the reminder. Employing deliberate repetition is more important for a book than for a film. Most readers don't read an entire book in one sitting; indeed, a reader can easily spend several weeks picking up and putting down a book.

Deliberate repetition can be employed in a broader, less concrete way, too, in order to resonate with the reader. For instance, if certain themes are central to your work, they might deliberately replay throughout. This is often used in psychological works, where the writer wants to, say, demonstrate the characters becoming like their parents. In *The Godfather*, the opening shot of the film—Don Corleone sitting in a chair—is subtly mimicked by the closing shot, of Michael Corleone sitting in a chair. The writer has employed deliberate repetition to show that the family has come full circle.

Character

Believe it or not, characters are created by context. A lead character is only a lead in relation to the other characters. If you have an ensemble cast of six people, all given equal time, there is no longer a single "lead." But if one of these is given one hundred pages, while each of the others is given only twenty, you now have a lead.

A character's significance must also be considered in context. Although the character with the most amount of pages (or stage time) is by default considered the "lead" character, as we mentioned earlier this doesn't necessarily mean he is the most significant character in the work (like Kurtz in *Heart of Darkness*). The significance of your character will also be determined in relation to the others. In context, Kurtz was most significant because the other characters all treated him as the most significant, as if he were a myth or a god; he was also, in context, the most unusual, since the other main characters were colonialists maintaining decorum, while Kurtz had forgone all restraint and lived among the natives.

Going back to our ensemble of six characters, even if all are given equal stage time, one of them might be considered more significant if, in context, this person is treated as most significant by the others—say, if he is considered the leader of the group, or if he is most unusual, e.g., if he is the only man among six women. In most cases, though, significance should come hand in hand with page time.

The impression your character makes will have a great deal to do with the context in which we meet him, or the context of the people he spends time with. If your character first comes onstage with three deadly gang members, his association with these people will affect our judgment. In fact, a gang is a perfect example of how context can be used to shape a character. If a character comes onstage by himself, he won't be feared; but if he comes onstage leading ten hardened criminals, he will be frightening. In this case, other characters are used to bolster our character. Likewise, other characters can detract from our character: If throughout the work he is a king surrounded by followers, but at the end he is by himself, we have watched our character fall simply within the context of the people around him (*Timon of Athens*).

Journey

If in a town full of white supremacists, one man goes against
the grain and befriends a black man, this man's journey will
stand out. However, if the entire town of white supremacists
befriends black men, then none of their journeys would stand
out. In this example, the effect of context is obvious; but you
must be conscious that you could dilute your main character's
journey by having another character take the same journey.

This is not to say that other characters in the work cannot
journey—on the contrary, they can and should. Others could,
though, take journeys that complement our protagonist's
journey. For instance, that town of white supremacists might,
at the same time, journey to becoming more violent and more
racist—this, in turn, would make our protagonist seem as if
he had journeyed even further from his ways. Or, conversely,
a group—such as a classroom of delinquents—might change
for the better, in which case if our character didn't journey
with them (even if he just stayed the same), he would, by
virtue of context, seem even more delinquent.

What could also obfuscate our character's journey in
context—although in a less direct and more mild way—is
other characters in that town taking different journeys, journeys which aren't the same as his but don't complement his
either—totally unrelated journeys—say, one becomes a father,
another gets divorced, etc. If one character journeys and the
others don't, he will be considered the most significant character, will be the one who stands out. A significant journey
signifies to the audience that this is *that* character's story. It
gives us the clue we've been waiting for to help us decide
whom to pay the most attention to, whom to follow, whom to

root for and care about, whom to be invested in; it entrenches us in a character's perspective and helps us sympathize.

Of course, each character has his own journey to make, but the thing to remember about journeys is that, when they're finished, you are left with a different character—so each journey doubles the number of characters in the work. The reader only has room for so many characters, and the more characters there are, the harder it becomes to give each attention.

Time

Most of us let the immediate past or immediate future affect our experience of the present; we live in the present in the context of the past and future. The same should hold true for your characters. Let's say your character buried his wife a week ago; perhaps he will walk around in a daze, be forgetful, cry in public; perhaps he will be angry, bitter, snap unexpectedly. He is still deep in mourning, and his present interactions must be considered in the context of his immediate past. Indeed, given the context of this man's immediate past, it would be unrealistic if this man were *not* in some way impacted (unless he is a cold murderer who killed his wife—in which case, his *not* reacting is itself significant).

This example is rather obvious, and most writers would take into account the context of such a dramatic situation. However, many writers might forget to take into account the context of this character's past after one year has passed, or two years, or ten. Might he have a sudden memory a year and a half later, and cry while on line at the supermarket?

Might he, three years later, visit a country inn he had stayed at with his wife and have a vivid memory and decide to leave? A death stays with you forever—as does nearly every significant event in the past. What is the cumulative effect of the life events on this character? When will the effects resurface? How?

A character can be equally preoccupied by the future, especially if a significant event is imminent. Let's say he is told he has one week to live—it would be hard for him *not* to live his life in the context of the future. Less drastically, let's say a woman has been preparing for her wedding for two years and it is now a week away. It is possible she will be anxious; perhaps she will snap, fight with her fiancée, her parents. Her present state of mind must be affected by the future.

Dramatic Irony

A woman leaves work on the dot at 5 P.M. every day, while her coworkers stay late. The boss dislikes her because of this, and decides he will never promote her. We, however, know she leaves at 5 P.M. because she has to take care of her dying parent, and the home nurse leaves at 5:30 sharp. Will the boss ever find out? Will she ever tell him? Will someone else? Will she never say a word and get fired? If he ever does find out, will he feel stupid, ashamed?

In a sense, dramatic irony is all about context. It is the excitement of watching a scene unfold with neither party knowing the context of the other person's life. It shows us what happens when people don't take context into account, and it is enjoyable for us to see how that always creates problems—often misunderstandings. It is the ultimate example that people and circumstances are impossible to understand without context.

Dramatic irony, in turn, helps create suspense. Let's examine this more closely below.

Suspense

Let's take a scene where a man and his wife are having lunch. There is nothing especially exciting about this. Now let's change it so that right before the man got there, he was called in by his boss and told he was fired. Now, as they have lunch, we wait to see if he will tell her or not; we anticipate what her reaction might be; we anticipate if there will be a scene. To further torture the audience, you can prolong this: You might have him begin to tell her several times, but then stop, or change the subject, or get cut off. By simply employing the context of this man's back story, we have taken an ordinary scene and made it suspenseful.

If you are going to use context in such a case, you have to realize its power and understand it will color the entire scene. The man, still in shock, is likely replaying the traumatic scene in his head. Perhaps he is spacey, perhaps he doesn't answer all of his wife's questions; perhaps he is more quiet than usual, or more talky. Perhaps he answers all of her questions in a false, chipper tone—or perhaps she asks him one thing, and he answers another. If she is truly his wife, she would know something's wrong; if she is just a blind date, she might, meeting him for the first time, think him odd.

One need also consider the context of suspense in the

work. If every single scene in the work has the audience on the edge of its seat, with no respite whatsoever, each scene will have less impact, and ultimately the audience will take the suspense less seriously. Conversely, if a work is slower throughout but then culminates in one single, suspenseful scene, that scene will not be forgotten. This is one of the reasons *Psycho* works. There is tension throughout, but scenes of true heart-pounding suspense are rare: There are only two—the shower scene and the final house scene. Additionally, they are spread far apart, so each can have its impact. If this work had, instead, shower scene after shower scene, *Psycho* would have become a B slasher movie, with little memorable suspense.

Conflict

Taking the same lunch story, we can see how context can also be used to create conflict. Perhaps the husband, just fired, shows up at the lunch angry and bitter; perhaps the wife just came from a fight with a colleague and is herself bitter. With such a setup, it won't be hard to create conflict at this lunch—even over nothing. Perhaps they argue over the menu, criticize each other, bring up old fights . . . Or let's say you had created the back story that his wife repeatedly threatened that if he got fired again she would leave him. Now, as they sit there eating, and he delays telling her, we cringe at the impending conflict.

In general, though, there needn't always be such high stakes to create conflict with context. All you need are two people coming from different places, in different states of mind. The husband who comes home from a ten-hour day exhausted, not feeling like dealing with anything, and the wife who had been waiting for him, alone, all day, and wants to talk. The context of their days puts them each in a different place, and, in a sense, pits each against the other.

As with suspense, a work cannot consist of conflict alone; one must take into account the context. There needs to be occasional respite, occasional resolve, for the conflict that does come to have greatest impact.

Setting

In Ray Bradbury's story "The Long Rain," a group of men are stranded on a planet where it rains incessantly. There is no shelter whatsoever, and the rain drives the men mad as they desperately search for a "solarium," a building that would provide relief. At the end of the story, the sole survivor finds it. After thirty pages of rain pounding on his head, he enters a building which is quiet, dry, warm, bright. The feeling of satisfaction this setting brings—both for the character and the reader—is exquisite. This is because of its context in the work, because of the miserable setting that preceded it.

As with everything else, context can have great impact on setting. A beautiful, sunny day by itself will seem unordinary; but after leaving a haunted house, a beautiful day will seem like paradise, and a character will revel in it. The ocean will seem ordinary for someone who lives on it; but for someone seeing it for the first time, it will seem miraculous. A family will be content in their four-room house, until they spend time in their friends' six-room house. Everything is relative, and to give a setting the greatest impact, consider preceding or following it with a setting that starkly contrasts it. A man goes from light into blackness; from a small prison cell to an opulent mansion; from shark-infested waters to the dry safety of a boat.

Great writers know this, and employ it frequently. Rare is the prison movie that begins and ends in a prison. Most prison works (*Shawshank Redemption, Escape from Alcatraz, An Innocent Man, Dead Man Walking*) begin and end *outside* of prison—or at least give us flashbacks to life outside prison; by framing the prison with normal life, it makes it, in context, more horrible. Works set in mental hospitals do the same; it is no mistake that in *One Flew over the Cuckoo's Nest* the protagonist takes his fellow inmates on an outing, or that the final shot of that film is of a character leaving the building.

Setting, working hand in hand with pacing and progression, also sets the stage for what the audience can expect. If 95 percent of the work takes place in one room, but then the last 5 percent of the work takes us through twenty settings, the work will feel disproportionate and the audience will feel jolted. Likewise, if the work takes us through a new setting every two minutes for 70 percent of the film, but then the last 30 percent takes place in one room, we will feel dissatisfied. If one setting is used too often, the audience can get restless; just as if the settings are constantly changing, we can become disoriented.

Pacing

If we are watching a war film and the first two acts are filled with action, the audience will get antsy if the final act comprises quiet dialogue between two people. However, if the first two acts had been a man sitting by himself, then dialogue between two people would be an acceleration of pace.

You must be careful about the pace you set, because with it you set the stage, and the audience will get used to it, demand similar pacing throughout. This especially holds true for action works—a fast pace means the audience is likely to get bored quickly if you take a break. With slower-paced works, the audience settles in; if you accelerate the pace too much too quickly, it will feel uneven.

At the same time, pacing is about contrast, and the audience needs an occasional break in the action. To maintain the fast pace, you need to give them a breather; to maintain the slow pace, you need to throw in some action. Be conscious of the context of the framework you're working in. This is a trap many beginning writers fall into: They open their works with extraordinary scenes that raise the bar, but then afterward take a step back, as they must, and slowly develop the work. If the opening scene is too fast-paced, it is nearly impossible to prevent the reader from getting antsy. Or, conversely, many writers will save all their action for the end, for one huge climax; but a scene like this will be impossible for the reader to take in after he has just been subjected to three slow-moving hours—he won't be in the mode to take in such a fast scene and won't absorb it. Better to start and end more evenly, and to spread it out in doses.

Progression

Progression and pacing are similar issues, yet pacing has to do with the speed at which the work is unfolding and progression has to do with whether it's leading somewhere at all. Just as the audience will get used to the pacing of the work, so will they get used to the progression. For instance, let's say by the end of Act I the protagonist has gone through a journey and is a completely changed person. This is a fast rate of progression, and thus the audience would expect a similarly high rate for the rest of the work. It won't suffice for your protagonist to just plod along, journeyless, at this point. You will need something equally progressive—either he'd need to slip all the way back to the bottom, or embark on a new journey. Or let's say the work is an action thriller, and in the first two hundred pages there has been much progression—war has been declared, submarines have been let loose, a fast-paced chase is in the works . . . If Act II then consists of a subplot that doesn't lead anywhere, the audience will become restless and dissatisfied.

If the work exhibits nothing but progress, we can feel no progress at all. It's like a car ride: If you slowly and steadily progress at ten miles an hour, you will hardly feel yourself moving and will take the progress for granted. But if you don't move at all for an hour and then suddenly you do fifty miles an hour, you feel your progress, although at the end of the day you end up at the same place. The same holds true for the audience: In the context of the work, slow and steady progress can be taken for granted, and sometimes stops and starts can make them appreciate progress more.

Meaning

Let's say two people get into a violent fight over a chess game. The next time they see a chessboard, tension will abound; it is not the board itself that creates the tension—it is the context of their relationship to it.

In a broader sense, the same holds true for a scene. In our lunch with the husband and wife, what you'll notice is that the scene is no longer about the lunch itself. The real focus of the scene is the context of what they bring to the lunch—his being fired, her fight with her colleague. They are so preoccupied that they will probably not remember a single detail about the lunch itself. When context is strong enough, it is as if the present moment is wiped out.

Likewise, although many writers don't realize it, context can (and often does) impact the overall meaning of a work. When finishing a work and reflecting on it, one finds that often the sheer weight of pages devoted to a certain topic or character will end up being what resonates. This has to do with allocation.

Far too often, writers don't stop to ask themselves: What is my work really about? How much space should be allocated to what? Is it about a character's rise, and if so, should I really be devoting 75 percent of the work to his downfall? Or is it about an event, in which case should I really wait until the halfway mark before getting to it? Is it about a relationship, in which case, should I be focusing so much on an unrelated event? How deeply one delves into any particular facet of a work will greatly affect its pacing, progression, focus, and ultimately its meaning.

Allocation is your master plan, and it, more than anything else, will be a reflection of what your story is about. Many writers plod ahead without making conscious decisions on space allocation; this is because many don't really know what their work is about until they've finished. There is nothing wrong with not knowing while writing. But once it's finished, the work must be shaped, and that usually means some writing must be cut, no matter how attached to it you are. Ultimately, decisions must be made, or else the work will end up disproportionate, weighted too heavily on topics, characters, events, or themes which ultimately are not central to its objective.

EXERCISES

Perspective

Editing for context has to do with first getting the proper perspective, a perspective that is hard, if not impossible, for you to get when you are too close to it. As a rule of thumb, when editing for context, the more time away before coming back to it, the better. Read the work through once, looking for context issues, such as repetition, and see what you find. Then set it down and come back to it two weeks later. What did you find this time that you didn't before?

Most writers, even with time away, have a hard time achieving perspective. This is inevitable. As a rule of thumb, try to give your work to at least one outside reader you can trust. What context issues did he find that you could not?

Repetition List

Take your list of characters and ask, which are similar? Do they detract from one another? Can one be cut? Can they be combined?

Make a list of your settings and ask, which are similar? Do they detract from one another? Can one be cut? Can they be combined?

Scene Transplant

Take a pivotal scene and transplant it to some other place in the work. If it comes at the beginning, move it to the end; if it comes at the end, move it to the beginning. What impact does this moving have on the work? How can context change the meaning of a scene? Are there any scenes you can transplant to other places?

Character Transplant

Take a character who is introduced early on and don't introduce him until later. Take a character who is introduced later and introduce him on page one. How does it change the work? How does context impact these characters? Are there any characters you should transplant to other places?

Allocation

Ask yourself, what is my work about? What are its main themes, characters, journeys? Now consider the work as a whole: Is the sheer number of pages in line with your mission? Have you allocated the bulk of your pages to characters, scenes, or issues of lesser importance? What might be cut? What can be added to bolster the original intention?

Chapter Eight

Transcendency

The greatest tragedian will also be the greatest comedian.
— SOCRATES

Maya Angelou once said she is not interested in facts, but truths. What is the difference? How can a work leave a deep, lasting impression on the audience, actually impact their lives?

Think of the some of the works that have stood the test of time, the books (*Moby Dick*), the plays (*Romeo and Juliet*), the films (*On the Waterfront*). If these had been relevant only to their place and time, they wouldn't have been embraced from one generation to the next. They prevailed because they all tapped universal, timeless truths and facets of the human condition.

Transcendency, when reduced, is primal. Although it is impossible to neatly label the effect, or to offer a formula, we'll look at some of the common elements of transcendent works, and see whether we can apply any of these to our own writing.

Character Multidimensionality

Although popular wisdom has it that every work needs a clearly defined hero and villain, you'll find that in many of the works that stood the test of time, the heroes and villains are not always so black-and-white. In *The Godfather*, the heroes are murderers; in fact, the one character who cannot bring himself to be violent—Fredo—is the one we respect the least. Often, in transcendent works, we love characters despite their faults, hate them despite their virtues. Perhaps this is because they remind us most of ourselves. This is the main point: not that they be good or bad, but that they be relatable. And since none of us is all good or all bad, it is more likely we will relate to characters who are, like us, a mix. The trick for the writer is figuring out how bad his hero can be, or how good his villain can be; some works, like *Silence of the Lambs*, come danger-ously close to crossing the line of sympathy, which can make for a huge hit—or a huge disaster. The answer is never easy.

The benefit of the multidimensional character, in addition to relatability, is that the character helps make the greater work open for interpretation; when everything is not quite so neatly wrapped up, the work becomes one which the audi-ence can reflect on, grapple with, debate over. It makes it a work they might want to experience again, especially given that, at different points in their lives, they might come to dif-ferent conclusions about the same characters.

Circumstance Multidimensionality

Often, having multidimensional characters is just a start; we also need to put them into situations and circumstances that test their mettle, which bring out their multidimensionality. Multidimensional circumstances take the burden off the characters' needing to perform, just as multidimensional characters take the burden off the circumstances needing to be morally complex. When the two converge, it can make for a powerful combination.

On an obvious level, a multidimensional circumstance might be A holding a gun to B's head and telling B that if he doesn't shoot C, he will be killed. For many, this would be a complex situation, and would elicit different reactions from different people. What is important is that the circumstance is so strong that it matters little how multidimensional B is— even if he is the most boring character, this scene will come alive.

The above example, while it illustrates a point, is hardly relatable, since very few people are confronted with such a circumstance in everyday life. The trick is to have multidimensional circumstances that might also occur in everyday life, which people can grapple with. You are on line at the supermarket and an old lady, who doesn't see you, cuts in front of you. She has many packages and will delay you fifteen minutes—and you are already late. Do you call her on it? Ask her to get behind you? It is a minor episode, but somehow these minor episodes can resound more compellingly than major ones. They are the stuff of everyday life, and our reactions seem to fill a giant, never-ending book of Precedent for Human Behavior. The more stories we hear, experiences we have, the more we fill in our own books; this is partly why we crave hearing others' stories, reading books or watching films at all. We are, in one sense, learning how to live.

Multidimensional circumstances help make a work transcendent, since they spark questions in the audience: "What would you do in that situation?" They help make it relatable, personal, ambiguous, create room for interpretation, and make the audience want to discuss it with others and perhaps see or read it again. If they raise a timeless and universal predicament, then there is an even greater chance the work might be embraced from one generation to the next.

Open to Interpretation

Many of the works that are canonized, that are assigned year after year in high schools and colleges, are assigned for precisely this reason: They are open for interpretation. If they were black-and-white, open-and-shut morality tales, it is hardly likely they would have lasted. This is why twenty students can write twenty different papers on a single work, all conflicting, and all equally valid. It is for this reason there are numerous schools of interpretation, from the New Historicists to the Deconstructionists. Indeed, graduate literature programs often spend more time focusing on the interpretation of the interpretation than on the works themselves.

Audiences return time and again to works kept open for interpretation, since these works can always challenge them, always spawn new ideas—they are like a mystery, and the satisfaction one receives is the satisfaction of completing a puzzle. The room for interpretation, though, should come in

the meaning, not with the basic facts or events; if the audience, on a basic level, cannot understand what transpires,
then the work will be merely confusing, not ambiguous. This
is a trap many beginning writers fall into.

Many writers, too, use their work being "open for interpretation" as a convenient excuse for not fully fleshing out
characters or events, not creating a fulfilling journey or
resolve. Interpretation does not come with lack of meaning. It
comes in abundance of meaning.

Multidimensional characters and circumstances open a
work for interpretation. So does its working on multiple levels. On a physical level, *Heart of Darkness* is about explo-
ration and shipping and an unknown continent; but it is also
a psychological work about a man gone mad; a sociological
work about colonialism and the brutality of civilization. The
more levels, the more there is to work with.

Timelessness

The colonialism in *Heart of Darkness* wasn't isolated to central Africa; it was taking place in many countries around the
world. *Heart of Darkness* was emblematic of an entire era. It
took a phenomenon of its time and spoke for its time; yet, at
the same time, it wasn't dated or temporal, since colonialism
had been occurring for thousands of years before and would
continue, in some form, for years to come. *Heart of Darkness*
captured the phenomenon by representing a snapshot, one
unique to the late 1890s (when Conrad wrote it) by way of its
steamships and focus on Africa and on ivory. He gave us the

particulars and individuality of the time without confining us to it.

For a work to be embraced from one generation to the next, there needs to be an element of timelessness; one way to make sure your work will *not* last is to make it particular to your time only. This is why many futurist films of the 1950s are now dated and forgotten (as they should be): they make "grand" predictions for the years 1970 or 1980 or 1990. In 1950 they might have worked, might have had everyone speculating over the year 1980. Now, in the year 2002, there is nothing left to speculate about, and no reason to watch the film.

The writer's task is to incorporate details of the time without making the work a product of the time. The play (and film) *Cabaret* does this skillfully. Set in Nazi Germany, it would have been easy to make the work solely about the Nazis and the state of things in Germany; instead, these remain in the background, and the film spends the bulk of its time on the romance and debauchery of Berlin in the 1930s. In the end the Nazis come to the forefront and interrupt the lives of the protagonists—but this doesn't come until the end, so we are able to slowly get the feeling of their coming into power. *Cabaret* uses the unique time of 1930s Berlin to make a timeless statement about humanity.

Ask yourself if the elements in your work are timeless. Would readers relate to its themes thirty years from now? Is there anything about it that might make it dated? At the same time, can you incorporate details of the time to bring it to life?

Relatability

The works that get translated into twenty-seven languages and are as big a hit in Japan as they are in Germany are works that are universal, that can be related to by all peoples. They are works that speak not to some element of the American condition—but to some element of the *human* condition. They are works that bring all peoples together through their universality, make them realize that human beings are the same everywhere, and make them feel a little less alone in the universe.

We are born into this world alone, and we must die alone. We ultimately have our own experiences, our own memories, and thus create our own, unique world—by default, every individual experience, every thought, every memory separates us from others. The more we live, the further from others we get, and the more we want to feel connected. We watch television, read the papers, attend parties, trying to feel a part of what others are doing, trying to feel "connected." This is why, even with the thousands of miles of uninhabited land on Earth, the vast majority of human beings choose to congregate in a few cramped cities, within a few square miles; why many human beings would rather sit in gridlock on Fifty-seventh Street in Manhattan blowing their horns than live peacefully in a remote landscape.

Despite our physical proximity to each other, most of us walk about feeling isolated. This is one of the reasons we turn to books, plays, films—to feel connected to others, to enjoy a collective experience. This is also why readers' groups and chat rooms and message boards pop up for us to further discuss a work—to make us feel even more connected. But the work must be the catalyst. Just as we want the shared experience with other people, with reading clubs, so we want the shared experience with the characters and circumstances in the work. There is nearly always some element of universality in works which last. Even a work like *The Castle,* where the characters and circumstances are so far out they are hardly relatable, the very inscrutability becomes something readers can relate to; indeed, the world "Castle-esque" has become a part of the lexicon, often used to refer to an inscrutable bureaucractic organization. The beginning writer tries so hard to be different, unusual, to stand out. But as he matures, he will find it is easy—and is also the greatest mistake. What is hard is creating a work with which an audience can deeply identify. These are the works that last.

Educational Element

Did you ever spend an entire night watching television, or spend a beautiful afternoon in a movie theater, and finish feeling guilty, like you've wasted your time, like you could have spent it more productively? There is a part of us that feels guilty about entertainment, whether through books, plays, films, or other media.

As a writer, one way to appease this is to add an educational element to your work. People love to learn, if in the right context. A viewer will feel less guilty having watched a one-hour show on the Discovery Channel about an animal he'd never heard of, or a show about new forensic detective methods he didn't know existed. Readers feel slightly less guilty reading Tom Clancy because they are also learning an incredible amount of technical information about warfare.

The educational element, particularly if never seen before, can give the work a feeling of substance and help elevate it to a work that will last.

To give your work that extra dimension, it should draw on some authentic area of life we don't know about, some subculture or specific topic. This will help ground it, bring it to life, and at the same time will educate—not in a textbook way, not by telling—but in a dramatic, natural way, by showing. It should prod us to consider some aspect of the world (or industry or class) we hadn't before. You may have heard that if you're writing a medical thriller, it's good to spend time with surgeons, to learn the names of instruments, the names of procedures, their protocols, their day to day—this not only educates the reader, but helps ground the work, make it authentic. Additionally, learning all these details might give you ideas for plot twists you hadn't considered before. That is what is meant by letting a work grow organically out of the research: Instead of imposing your story on the research, the research tells you what your story should be.

By education I don't mean merely dropping facts (which are usually forgotten), but showing an entire world. The best works don't focus all the attention on this world, but let it reside comfortably in the background. Consider *The Deer Hunter*. It uses the subculture of blue-collar, Pittsburgh steel miners, a world which few people know much about; yet the story is not about Pittsburgh steel but about Vietnam and friendships. Consider *The Chosen*. It teaches us about the ultra-orthodox Hasidic Jewish world; yet it is not about a boy who wants to become a rabbi, but rather about a boy who wants to leave that world.

Self-discovery

Great writing leads us to look inside. It makes us feel not only educated, but also self-aware, enlightened. This is why some works—the very best—will make someone feel like a changed person for having experienced it.

The road to self-discovery is the road to relatability, but with a sharp fork—at some point there is some unpredictable element that makes the audience consider a path they never have before. This is the point where writers will either lose relatability or coax the audience toward some insight of their own. It is a scary moment for the writer, as it requires a leap of faith from the audience, and there are never any guarantees, since this is a journey every reader or viewer must decide upon for himself. But there are few things more gratifying for an audience than coming to a self revelation as a result of reading or watching a work.

Lasting Impression

Transcendent works leave a deep, lasting impression on the reader, and can become an integral part of his psyche. Did you ever think of a person and wonder where you'd met him, only to realize you'd never met him, that he was a character in a book, play, or film? Characters—and entire works—can become so integrated into your psyche that the memories can feel as if they are your own.

One goal for the writer is to speak to the audience's subconscious, which would assure that the work is remembered not just intellectually but viscerally. One way to do this is through the use of symbolism, imagery, and metaphor. There are, for instance, a powerful series of icons—from the spider to the sun—that have taken on meaning over thousands of years and will speak to the audience in a primal way. You can incorporate psychological, sociological, mythological, and philosophical icons and allusions. You can allude to other works. Shakespeare's plays are filled with biblical allusions. Imagery often resonates with us on some deep level. Maybe this is what will bring us back to the work, make us want to read it again, talk about it with others; perhaps we won't even like it the first time, but will be inexplicably drawn back.

Works that leave lasting impressions are usually greater than the sum of their parts. The greatness lies not in any individual character, or setting, or story twist, but in the coming together of these elements. It is like a soup: Individually, the water is just water and the carrots are just carrots and the garlic is just garlic; but, in their totality, we have a soup. What is the overall impression the work makes? Is it inspiring? Devastating? What about it could make one want to return to it? What about it might instill it into the reader's psyche?

Transcendency Pitfalls

Although it is crucial to consider what elements comprise a lasting, transcendent work, and to try to incorporate these elements in your own work, the elements must be organic—they cannot be manufactured. While one must strive for greater purpose and meaning, one must also be careful of forcing it. This is a trap many beginning (and advanced) writers fall into, in various forms. Below, we consider a few.

Works that push for profundity. Much of today's so-called "literary" writing—coming out of modern MFA programs, published in literary journals, by literary presses or imprints—is weak on plot. It is assumed that the writing's being well crafted, line by line, is enough; that if the sentences are pretty enough, plot is incidental. But since there is no real plot, no real suspense or conflict or momentous journey, the writers have to compensate somehow. Often they try to make up for it by hinting, through minimalism or symbology or metaphor, at a deeper meaning that simply doesn't exist. They'll consistently leave paragraphs and chapters dangling with mysterious sentences, with lack of resolve, as if to intimate some greater truth. You must realize, though, that profundity comes from characters and circumstances, and cannot be imposed. If they changed their priorities so that a suspenseful plot was foremost, they would no longer feel the need to push for meaning.

Writing with an agenda. When someone writes with an agenda, the audience will always see through it. The work will be stale, flat, the characters and circumstances won't come alive. This is because the writer, by definition, is imposing his vision on the work, instead of letting the vision grow organically from it. Also, he is touting his doctrine, his point of view, and doing little more than proving a point. There is another term for these types of works: propaganda. There is no room for propaganda in creative writing. Indeed, creative writing is the enemy of propaganda, since it can never be controlled and has no hidden agenda whatsoever.

Morality Tales. As much as your writing is a work of art, it can also be a vehicle, a platform for your message. This becomes shockingly clear when you reach millions of people and, as a result of your writing, popular culture is influenced, people go out and take action. You learn you have a responsibility, whether you impact one million lives or just one. You become more than just an entertainer, an artist—you become a teacher, a role model. Being published—or being produced—is a privilege. What is your message? What action might the audience take as a result?

Still, as important as it is to know your message, you must remember that you are ultimately an artist, not a moralist. As an artist, your goal is to dramatize, to bring to life—not to state facts or propound an agenda. Works that strive to put forth a moral or teach a lesson will generate resentment in the audience. It is actually a variation of writing with an agenda, and is still contrived. Such writing is suited for fairy tales, children's stories, and biblical lessons, but has no place in creative writing. Such a work leaves no room for spontaneity or improvisation.

Transcendency is not formulaic, and there are no rules or steps to guide you; by its very nature, it cannot be manufactured. Still, one must make the effort and, in addition to pondering the above elements, below are some more practical issues to consider:

The Audience Arc

The ideal work takes the audience through four stages:

Curiosity. Every reader and viewer goes through this stage: Whoever picks up a book or goes to a movie is curious. Getting this far is a gift: It means sales and marketing people have done their job for you and done it well; it means the word has gone out far enough that a complete stranger could be drawn to your work; and it means the work has been distributed widely enough that someone can logistically read or see it. It means a stranger could devote two or three hours (or in the case of a book, perhaps two or three weeks!) of his precious time solely to giving you a chance on your creation. Now it is your turn to reciprocate.

Interest. At this stage—which not all readers or viewers reach—the audience is intrigued by your characters and circumstances. They have no intention of walking out of the theater, and if someone turned off the light while they were reading or changed the channel while they were watching, they would get annoyed. They want to see where it goes. However, they are not totally hooked yet. They are interested, perhaps even hooked, but don't *need* to see it through.

Need. Fewer works reach this stage. This is the stage where, if someone were to shut off the TV, the viewer would *need* to know how it ended; he would run out immediately and rent the video. It is not a fleeting need—such as needing to know who the killer is—since this type of need, while strong in the short run, rarely resonates with the viewer. It is a need on every level, a point where the work has created such strong characters and circumstances, initiated so many journeys, created such a lack of resolution, earned deep sympathy, and made the audience utterly relate to the character, that it is as if they are watching their own lives play out. If they haven't seen it to the finish, they feel as if their own lives hang in the balance.

Action. Very few works reach this stage. The highest level to which you could rouse the audience is a place where they are so moved by the work that merely finishing it or leaving the theater is not enough; you have instilled in them a burning desire to take action based on what they've read or seen. The work has deeply moved them. Perhaps you've inspired them to do something they had never had the courage to do; perhaps you've shown them some indignity of which they were unaware and have infuriated them. There are, of course, varying levels of taking action, from resolving to do something, to writing a letter to Congress, to leaving the theater and starting a riot. In Shakespearean times, all plays required approval of the King; the authorities knew that nothing has the power to incite the masses as much as literature. We even witness this today, as the Rodney King tapes (and trials) sparked riots across the country, as films like *JFK* sparked thousands of letters to Congress and forced secret files finally to be opened. This is the ultimate power you wield as a writer. You have the power not only to change a mind, to convince anyone of something he thought inconceivable, but to actually incite him to act based on it.

Ask yourself (and ask five other readers): does my work

inspire curiosity, interest, need, or action? Does it achieve all four levels? Why or why not? On a scale of 1 to 10, where does it fall? What can be changed to help accomplish this?

Emotion

One way to help you arouse interest, need, and incite the audience to action is to stir the audience's emotions. Emotions are intuitive, and are much more powerful than reason. This is why it is said that good speakers appeal to the intellect and great speakers appeal to the emotions. It is not uncommon for a leader to win a debate—or even an election—who is intellectually inferior to his opponent but is better able to incite the emotions of the masses. Indeed, this is precisely why Hitler was able to get as far as he did: Although his message was complete nonsense, he was still able to appeal to emotions, to stir crowds into a frenzy. Martin Luther King and other great preachers also knew this and provoked emotion; this is why in their speeches they'll often stop and repeat a powerful line a few times.

Consider the many romances (and soap operas) that are nearly substanceless but nonetheless appeal to the emotions and propel the audience to finish. Consider the slasher movies that have the audience so clouded by fear that they lose their reason long enough to realize that what they are watching is empty. Consider stand-up comedy where a crowd will laugh for hours over fluff. Yet readers will *willingly*, time and again, come back to works they *know* are substanceless if they also know they will be adequately moved to sadness, fear, or laughter. It is not by accident that many of the more emotive mediums—the hilariously funny comedies, the tear-jerking romances—tend to be light on substance; in some ways, they are incompatible, as emotion clouds reason, and substance demands reason.

The beginning actor is taught never to go for the emotion; if one enters a scene saying "I am going to cry" or "I am going to be angry," then one's emotion is bound to be manufactured, false. The preferred method is to use your imagination to commit to the circumstance of the scene, to put yourself in the moment. If the circumstance is strong enough and you commit yourself deeply enough, you should, organically, be moved to cry, moved to anger. The same holds true for writing. If your intention is to provoke emotion, you can't go about it by telling the reader "You should be sad now;" instead, you need to create the characters and circumstances that will organically move your readers to be sad. But also ask yourself, why move the reader to this particular emotion? What do you hope to gain? How will it impact the work?

An ancillary benefit of creating a work with strong emotional impact is that it creates a lack of resolution. The angry character lacks resolution: He eventually needs to calm down. The crying character lacks resolution: He eventually needs to stop crying. Even a person in a state of euphoria must eventually come back down. Emotions are, by their nature, temporal. The greater the emotion, the greater the need for resolution. Wildly emotional people always need to have resolution, which is why it's exhausting to be around them. It's also exciting, because they are unpredictable— indeed, unpredictability is an ancillary benefit of having emotional characters in a work.

A good question to consider is, when we come back to "normal"—from crying or a fit of anger or euphoria—what is "normal"? What is our natural state of emotion? What about the person who never shows emotion? Wouldn't he be considered strange? Then again, the man who walks about his office alternately weeping and in fits of rage could also be considered strange. It seems society wants us to show *some* emotion, at the proper times, although as a rule of thumb seems to be more tolerant of those who show no emotion than those who do: No eyebrows would be raised if a man left a sad film with a dry face, but people would look twice if a man cried at an ice-cream store if they didn't have his flavor. What is your character's normal state? How prone is he to show emotion, on a scale of 1 to 10? Which emotions is he inclined to show? Anger? Sadness? Euphoria? Which emotions does he hide? How does he compensate for hiding his emotions?

Your Conscious Motivation

A question of great value which many writers never consider is, why are you writing? What is your motivation? It is an elemental question, but the most overlooked. Are you writing to make them laugh? To scare? To educate? To entertain? To incite to anger? The answer "I write because I have to" doesn't suffice here. This is about the reader. Indeed, this is precisely the problem: Most writers don't consciously consider how they hope to move the reader. If you can fully achieve this state of selflessness, then direction, tone, style, story then will fall into place.

In many cases, the impetus for your writing might not be a

conscious motivation. You might have been struck with a great idea, or an idea for a great character, and just began writing. If such is the case, work backward. Look at what you've done, at what's on the page, or consider your idea, and analyze it. Is it depressing? Uplifting? Dark? Light? Why this story? What has attracted you to it? By working backward, you can begin to get a handle on your conscious motivation, on your own sensibility. Knowing your own *modus operandi* is empowering: It puts you in control, instead of being at the whim of your instincts.

Goal for the Work

Once you are clear about what you're setting out to achieve, you can proceed with more clarity and confidence, and also be able to step back and hone what you've done with more of a bird's-eye view. It will be easier to let go of drafts, to cut what exists, and write new sections. When you are truly able to go back to the source, you inherently distance yourself from what's on the page.

The problem with writing, as an art form, is that it is more difficult for the artist to let go. The actor tries something and it doesn't work, and he simply tries something else; the potter tries something and doesn't like it and simply collapses the clay. For a writer, though, a mere draft of a novel can take years, so it's less easy to just scrap it and try something else; on the contrary, it's easier for writers to find reasons to justify why what they've already done is good. Thus writers spend most of their time trying to make a bad draft work instead of coming up with a new draft. In one sense, the chief task of the writer is to stay unattached and not to let ego get involved. Returning to your original goal and motivation helps you achieve this.

Your Unconscious Motivation

Your unconscious motivation will show in the writing, and will be what ends up resonating with the audience. Stop for a moment and check in with yourself, on the deepest level. What place are you coming from when you write? For instance, are you writing from a place of defensiveness? Insecurity? To prove a point? If so, you might overcompensate by assuming the reader is in disagreement with you and arguing points that don't need to be argued. There is aggression in proving a point on the page, just as there is aggression in proving a point in real life. Such writing ends up fighting the reader rather than connecting with him, and can be off-putting. Are you writing from a place of pride? Needing to prove your intellect? If so, you might overcompensate with high language, abundant references, and affected terms, which could make the work more a showcase for you and your writing, and keep the reader at a distance. Are you writing from a place of fear? This, too, can show through in the writing: You could be afraid to declare things, end up backing everything up three times. Are you writing to control the reader? If so, you might end up mapping everything out methodically, trying to force the same reading experience on everyone, and you will also end up with little spontaneity or improvisation. Are you writing for revenge? Are you writing a tell-all, or a *roman à clef*, or basing a character on someone you know in real life? This, too, can come through, since your agenda for revenge will keep you from being true to the work, from changing the characters or story if need be. Are you writing from a place of deception? The audience will intuit you are telling only part of the story, and your half-truths will hold you back from creating a well-rounded work.

As a writer, your mind is your palette, and unfortunately your mind stores a lot of baggage. It is your job to clear the slate, to create a sacred space in your mind just for the writing, free from all your neuroses as a person. The writing must be about the art as much as possible. You must clear your mind of pride, defensiveness, the urge to control, to write with an agenda, or to hold anything back.

No matter what your goal or motivation, you should strive to write from a place of truth and love. This sounds simple but is harder than it seems, as it will entail putting yourself on the line. "Truth" means being true to yourself and true to your characters and situations; if you hold anything back, the reader will know it; it will mean the difference between authentic and inauthentic. As a writer, consider yourself under oath. Be prepared to plumb the depths of a character, to bring out every last thought in his psyche—no matter how ugly—or don't introduce him at all. "Love" means not only love for the reader but love for your own work, your own characters; it means having 100 percent passion for them. Even with a character as sinister as Hannibal Lecter, we can feel the love, the passion the writer has for him, and a part of us can't help loving him, too. Passion is magnetic. Writing from a place of truth and love, you can never go wrong.

I can always tell the difference between a writer who writes because he wants to and one who writes because he *has* to. Flannery O'Connor's words burn with life; the intensity is overwhelming and cannot be ignored. She battled a terrible disease throughout her short life and knew her days were numbered. For her writing wasn't an idle way to pass the time, but literally a matter of life and death. It wasn't for many years until I came across writing that mirrored hers for intensity. It was the writing of a man named Donald Rawley, who, as it turned out, was in the final stages of a fourteen-year battle with HIV. I wasn't surprised. The words burned with an authenticity and desperation that would have been impossible to fake, and his books make for some of the greatest modern literature.

Great writers are desperate. For them, every sentence is a matter of life and death, just as for the great samurai every battle was a matter of life and death. You needn't be dying or imprisoned, but you do need to tap that part of yourself that has driven you to write in the first place. When you have done so, you will know it. You will no longer be writing because you like to, but because you *need* to. And if a day should pass when you skip your writing, you will feel it viscerally, as if you've skipped a dose of medicine.

Conclusion

What is a transcendent work? Is it one that receives critical acclaim, prestigious awards? One that sells millions of copies, is embraced by the masses? One that stands the test of time, lasts from one generation to the next? It is hard to say. I know many writers who receive the acclaim but not the sales and are despondent and feel like they've failed; I know many more writers who receive the sales but not the acclaim, and feel unworthy. I know other writers who have had an individual work last over time, but not others, and feel as if they perhaps have only one good work in them.

Ultimately, each is a unique accomplishment in its own right, and none should be judged against the other. The masses are fickle, and so are the critics. You mustn't pay attention to any of it, but simply stay focused on crafting the best work you can, and constantly bettering yourself. Ultimately, you must be your own judge: The transcendent work is the work you know is the best you can offer. And your offering, in and of itself, is an act of transcendency.

Stories are necessary. Like food or water, stories have always been of supreme importance to the human race. They speak to us on a primal level, and they fill a need. Life can seem aimless, structureless, unjust, without resolution. Stories are the antidote to life: they offer purpose, structure, justice, resolution—not to mention romance, suspense, conflict, adventure. They offer meaning. If our lives cannot always have it, our stories can.

Stories in all forms—novels, screenplays, memoirs, plays, poems—can change lives. They can motivate, inspire, offer an enhanced sense of life, an example of how to live. They can provide a means of escape—from our lives or for a despondent prisoner. They can heal, provide a catharsis, captivate a bedridden child, make him forget his pain. They can educate, instigate, even incite to revolution. They can bring people together. And they can tear them apart. They can poison; works like *Mein Kampf* can spread hatred and misinformation, and brainwash. Stories have been glorified, preserved for thousands of years. They have also been censored, repressed. There is some magical element in storytelling, something mysterious that we'll never label. It is the most powerful form of human creation. It is thought on the page, and few things of this Earth are more powerful than thought.

It all lies before you on the blank page. From your mind to your hands to the keys. Nothing is stopping you from changing the world.

Epilogue

Many books on plot emphasize the prem-
ise or idea; you'll find many books talking about the "twenty
master plots" or "thirty-six fundamental storylines." These
books are a necessary contribution, and the importance of
the idea is not to be dismissed. However, many writers today
believe that concept is all-important, that merely having a
good concept will mean success, and that without it all is lost.
This book has set out to show that that isn't the case. A great
premise can fall apart without proper execution, and what
seems to be a lesser story can come to life magnificently if
unfolded properly.

The subtitle mentions eight ways. The first three are characterization (the outer life, the inner life, and applied); these
show how your characters, if examined in depth, can give

you ideas for story. The journey emphasizes the characters' arcs, destinations, which will in turn give your work a sense of progression. Suspense and conflict will keep the journey lively, give it the texture it needs for the long, middle stretches. Context will help you shape the work as a whole. And transcendency will prod you to create a work of greater meaning. It is one approach, and if worked with carefully, will yield results. You should learn from it, then make it your own. Or, as Nietzsche said, "The artist must first be the camel, bearing the weight of schooling. He must then become a lion, and destroy his teachers."

Why a book on plot at all? Why not a book on style, or dialogue? Aren't they equally important? Yes, they are, but each is deserving of a book (if not many books) in its own right, which is why my first book, *The First Five Pages*, was devoted to style, and why my next one will be devoted to dialogue. Then why plot?

The question is more easily answered by looking at a work which lacks plot. We encounter these frequently: films which have beautiful settings, wardrobe and props, books which have pretty prose, yet in which nothing *happens*. Despite all the merits—which could be considerable—we leave feeling empty. We haven't witnessed something happen. We haven't witnessed change.

Plot, more than anything, is the enemy of stasis. Plot demands people dying and being born; getting married and divorced; saving lives and murdering. Something—no matter how small—must change. It is your job to create instability, and then, perhaps, to set it right.

A book on plot compels us to remind ourselves, repeatedly, to create instability. Without such reminder, even the most advanced writers can inevitably fall prey to stasis. Characters, journey, suspense, conflict, transcendency—each chapter is designed to foster change. With every change, your work will become something else. As it does, it will leave behind a trail of progression points. Each point is a marker on the road to plot. Each point brings you one step closer to bringing your fiction to life.

Appendix A

Suggested Reading and Viewing

On Writing in General (a select list, alphabetical by author)
Beyond the Writer's Workshop by Carol Bly
Characters & Viewpoint by Orson Scott Card
How to Write a Damn Good Novel by James Frey
The Key: How to Write Damn Good Fiction Using the Power of Myth by James Frey
Dynamic Characters by Nancy Kress
The Craft of Writing the Novel by Phyllis Reynolds Naylor
Creating Unforgettable Characters by Linda Seger
The Craft of Writing by William Sloane
20 Master Plots by Ronald Tobias

On Language (a select list, alphabetical by author)
The Lexicon by William F. Buckley, Jr.
Sleeping Dogs Don't Lay by Richard Lederer, Richard Dowis
Words Fail Me by Patricia O'Connor
Elements of Style by William Strunk, Jr. and E.B. White
Word Count by Barbara Wallraff

Miscellaneous on Writing (a select list, alphabetical by author)
Advice to Writers by Jon Winokur
Rotten Reviews edited by Pushcart Press

Classic Literature (a select list, alphabetical by author)
The Stranger by Albert Camus
Heart of Darkness by Joseph Conrad
The Idiot by Fyodor Dostoyevsky
The Castle, Complete Stories by Franz Kafka
Moby Dick by Herman Melville
Everything That Rises Must Converge by Flannery O'Connor
The Narrative of A. Gordon Pym by Edgar Allan Poe
Julius Caesar, Coriolanus, Macbeth by William Shakespeare

Modern Literature (a select list, alphabetical by author)
[Disclaimer: Many of these works are written by novelists I represent.
They are also works I'd recommend, since I, naturally, wouldn't rep-
resent fiction I didn't feel passionately about.]
Among the Missing by Dan Chaon
The Old Ballerina by Ellen Cooney
Wake of the Perdido Star by Gene Hackman and Daniel Lenihan
Having Everything by John L'Heureux
Here in the World by Victoria Lancelotta
Circumnavigation by Steve Lattimore

The River Warren by Kent Meyers
A Compendium of Skirts by Phyllis Moore
The Night Bird Cantata, Tina in the Back Seat by Donald Rawley
American Son by Brian Ascalon Roley
Cold by John Smolens
Nude in Tub by G. K. Wuori

Classic Films (a select list, alphabetical by title)
A Clockwork Orange
Apocalypse Now
Blade Runner
Cabaret
The Chosen
Das Boot
The Deer Hunter
Deliverance
The Dinner Game
Dog Day Afternoon
Driving Miss Daisy
The Empire Strikes Back
Fitzcarraldo
Five Easy Pieces
The Gift
The Godfather I and *II*
I Never Sang for My Father
Invasion of the Body Snatchers
Klute
Lawrence of Arabia
Manhunter
Network
North by Northwest

On the Waterfront
One Flew over the Cuckoo's Nest
Psycho
Rocky I and II
The Shining
Scarface
Serpico
Shakespeare in Love
Silence of the Lambs
Sling Blade
Snatch
Spartacus
Stepford Wives
Straight Time

Appendix B

Internet Resources

E-Mail Lists
Publishers Lunch (free) (www.caderbooks.com)
PW Rights Alert (www.PublishersWeekly.com)

Websites (a select list)
www.PublishersWeekly.com
www.PublishersMarketplace.com
www.bookwire.com
www.imdb.com
www.writersdigest.com
www.pw.org
www.prairieden.com
www.authorlink.com

www.bookzone.com
www.rosedog.com
(also see *Writer's Digest*'s annual issue for the "101 Best Websites for Writers")

About the Author

Noah Lukeman is president of Lukeman Literary Management Ltd, a literary agency based in New York, which he founded in 1996. His clients include multiple winners of the Pulitzer Prize, American Book Award, Pushcart Prize, and O. Henry Award; finalists for the National Book Award, Edgar Award, and Pacific Rim finalists; multiple *New York Times* bestsellers; national journalists; major celebrities; and faculty members from universities ranging from Harvard to Stanford. He has worked as a manager in the New York office of Artists Management Group, Michael Ovitz's multi-talent management company, and, prior to becoming an agent, on the editorial side of several publishers and as editor of a literary magazine. He is author of the bestselling *The First Five Pages: A Writer's Guide to Staying Out of the Rejection Pile,* now part of the curriculum in many universities.

If you wish to contact the author or comment about this book, you may visit its dedicated website:

www.lukeman.com/theplotthickens